God's
Notebook

God's Notebook

Fay Davidson

ISBN: 978-1-4269-4574-8 (sc)
ISBN: 978-1-4269-4614-1 (e)

Trafford rev. 02/14/2011

 www.trafford.com

North America & international
toll-free: 1 888 232 4444 (USA & Canada)
phone: 250 383 6864 ♦ fax: 812 355 4082

Foreword

God's Notebook is a providential tool, challenging the nominal believer, encouraging the challenged child of God, enabling the searcher for truth, and impacting those tending towards skepticism.

This book is an instrument for a devotional understanding of the perSon of God. *God's Notebook* is a reflection of the mind of God as revealed in the scriptures. Its textual accuracy and doctrinal purity is often hidden in the simple readable conversational dialogue.

God's Notebook bridges the gap between the academic biblical, theological research of the scriptures on the perSon of God, and the light pedestrian, irreverent approach that is commonplace in today's Christian community.

May each reader's heart be warmed, their mind challenged, and their life changed as they meet the God of the scriptures, through this medium.

Fay, thank you for the privilege of vetting and commenting on this work. May its impact extend far beyond your expectations to divine horizons.

Rev. Milton Davidson
Pastor, Pitfour Church of God
Montego Bay, Jamaica

Contents

I Am 1

Never-ending Kingdom.....................................3

You Have Rejected Me 6

Self and My Kingdom..9

My Word is Life 12

No Delight 15

Family Tree 17

Peace with Persecution 19

A Nurturing Kingdom 23

No Midway 26

Two Kingdoms..30

Full Obedience 31

The Eagle 36

A New Heart 39

One Way into My Kingdom.............................42

Truth and My Kingdom 46

Kingdom of Mammon or God 47

Faith and My Kingdom...................................49

Faith in My Kingdom 52

Love and Justice..55

An Open Door...58

Real Life 60

I Delight in your work.....................................62

I Need Your Heart 64

If I Change 66

Conversations 69
I Am Always There 72
My Kingdom is Infinite 74
Disappointments 76
I Never Sleep 78
Waiting 80
God of the Marketplace 83
Perseverance 86
New Beginnings 87
Time for Me 89
Eternal Laws 92
Beware of Deception 94
Nirvana 97
Test Administrator 100
Parables 102

I Am

I am God who made you and the earth in which you live. I made all the planets and the other worlds around you along with the trees and rocks and precious stones: gold, silver, diamonds ... even oil and gas. I made it all for you and me.

But I assure you that you are the centre of the visible universe. You, mankind, are the zenith of my creation on earth. You, whom I made in my own image and likeness, are the only creature I have given the ability to think, reason, and speak. You are the ones to whom I have given the ultimate distinction of superior life form, language and choice. You are the apple of my eye and the centre of my world.

Before I explain my desire and my purpose for you, I will reveal the depths of my heart to you. *I LOVE YOU.* I love you more than you can ever imagine or dream of ... I love you with all the depths of my being. I love you eternally, forever. My love for you cannot change, nor can it be measured: its bearing cannot be known. In the same way I cannot be fathomed because I am God, so you cannot fathom my love, until we meet face to face in my realm, when my Kingdom is fully established here on earth.

Believe me that I love you, even when you don't understand, even when everything around you seems to say: 'It cannot be;

surely Love cannot do this. Love cannot allow such tragic things to come to pass. Love must step in and stop this madness.

And even when Love seems silent amidst all the evil and chaos around you, and even when your own life seems in shambles, and you feel you have lost focus and direction, you must trust me. You still must believe that I love you … in spite of. In spite of anything, and everything, *I LOVE YOU* and do not desire to see you hurt.

I know it is hard for you to grasp or believe this. But I ask of you, the zenith of my creation on earth, that you trust me and believe in me, even if not for my sake, then for your own good. You will understand … eventually.

Never-ending Kingdom

My kingdom is an everlasting kingdom. It existed before the beginning of time and will persist to the end of this age and for all eternity. My kingdom came into being the same moment I came into existence, and I am the eternal I Am. I am without beginning or ending, and so is my kingdom.

The essence of my kingdom cannot be perceived with the natural eye, as my kingdom is both visible and invisible. I dwell in the heaven of heavens far above the earth and every created thing. The kingdom that is invisible to your eye is a city with streets paved with gold and adorned with the most precious of gems. It is peopled with angels and archangels, cherubim and seraphim, and with mansions of saints who have passed through this earth, and have joined the heavenly host. But my kingdom also resides within you – those of you know me.

I am one God but manifested in three persons – Father, Son and Holy Spirit – just as you are one, but consist of body mind and spirit. As Father, I sit on my throne in heaven, and from my mind has emanated all of creation. Jesus, the Son, gave up his glory and put on flesh to come down to earth and die that you might reclaim the eternal life I intended for you at the beginning. Jesus completed his assignment and is now sitting at my right hand making intercession for you. The third person of the Godhead, the Holy Spirit resides on earth, as heaven's representative to teach the culture of my kingdom and to instruct you in my ways.

I have always resided in the heavens, and the earth I singularly designed to be my footstool – the place above all of my creation, where I choose to inhabit, and make my rest. Of the entire universe, I chose to people, planet earth. My intent was, and still is, to create a nation of kings and priests with authority to rule the land through the counsel and instruction of my Spirit.

I wanted a people of peace and beauty who I would commune with daily – a people who would seek to know my heart and the things that pleased me. A people who would embrace my Holy Spirit, listen to his instructions and follow his counsel.

I wanted a people who managed with integrity, the resources and ideas I gave to them. I wanted them to love me, to refer to me, to understand me, and draw close to me. I wanted them to know that in me lay their ability to live life to the fullest. In me was their capacity to be creative and happy, and to experience peace. In me alone was their ability to prosper and to rule successfully the land I gave to them. In me would be their life, their hope, and their true sustenance. In me was everything they would ever want or ever desire. But they rejected me.

They didn't understand that I did not want them to defer to me for selfish reasons: they didn't understand that it was not that I wanted to restrict them and control them and their movements. They did not understand that it was because I wanted the best for them. I wanted them to be happy and fulfilled, and to have life … eternal life. I wanted them to be near me and share my joy, but they would not. They did not understand that in me alone could they find all the things they were seeking for. They refused to believe me.

They thought that I was altogether a liar as they are: they chose to believe a lie above the truth which they first heard from me, and since then, their teeth have been set on edge to believe lies. They have resented me – and coveted my authority and power, and they have sought, like the Evil One, to defy me and usurp my position and rule. They do not know; they don't understand that I made them, and it cannot be so. Man cannot take my place … man cannot overthrow me.

I am God; I am the beginning, the middle and the ending. I exist alone, without need of any other life to sustain me. I am God alone and there is none beside me. I reign supreme all by myself. I am a God of love, but one thing I cannot and will not do: I will not share my glory with another. I am to be feared, I am to be treated with awe and dread. I am the creator of all things: in me dwell all things. I am life itself and I will not take away from myself to submit to my own creation.

You Have Rejected Me

My creation, the ones in whom I have placed my very own spirit, has rejected me. The ones, who I placed in control of the life I created on earth, have chosen to be their own god, and to claim ownership of the things I created for their use and their glory.

How can they not understand that I love them – that I gave my very life for them? How can they not know me when there is evidence of me all around for them to see? If they want to know me, they can see me.

I am for you, not against you; I love you, not hate you; I desire you, not spurn you. Why can't you understand what is good for you, what is to your own benefit? Why don't you trust me? You are my own. I bought you back with a price – the price of my own life. Why don't you turn to me and trust me? I have loved you with my life. I came down to reach out to you, but you still rejected me – you in whom I placed my own heart and spirit.

I cannot help but love you because you are a part of me. You are my own flesh and blood, yet you will not have me. Turn to me, turn to me and love me, for I am your own … your very own who died for you … who gave his life for you. Turn to me, for I love you dearly. I gave you my own life and breath.

I cannot bear to see you in pain … hurting, tossing without sleep at night. I see you and my heart goes out to you, but I can't help you because you won't turn to me or call out to me. I stand in your room and see your grief and agony, and want to help you, but can't because you won't look up to see me or stretch out your hand to me. If only you could see my heart of love and compassion, reaching out in longing for you. But I can't help you because I am a just God, a holy God, a God of integrity. I cannot break my word and give you help unless you ask, or I would become like you, a covenant-breaker.

I said from the beginning that you should call out to me and I would answer, and that is what I mean. When you call I will answer: I always do. But I can't intrude in your life on my own because I gave you a free spirit to choose. That was my covenant with you when I made you like myself – you would choose to live the way you wanted. You would choose your life. However, I made it clear to you, at the time, what the consequence of your choice would be. I told you outright what death was – that you would die if you became separated from me. You understood, but you chose otherwise … you made your choice.

In spite of my forthrightness … in spite of what I said, you somehow felt you were choosing life above death when you chose to disobey me. But death is bound up in disobedience; death comes with disobedience. Death is born of disobedience. So I counsel you, choose life.

Even now, choose life for yourself and your family. In me alone is life, your life. There is no other life outside of me. Don't you understand, I am the only source of life? Everything outside of me is death. That is what I have been trying to tell you all this time. Life is in me alone. I myself am life; I personify life. I cannot help you if you do not choose me … if you do not choose life.   If you do not choose me then you have chosen death voluntarily. Choose life, I still plead with you: choose life in me.

Without me, you are alone in the world … alone on your own, struggling against all the evil powers of darkness when you disobey and choose death. You struggle, and then die because you turn from me. You experience pain and death with no reprieve when you turn from me.

So turn to me, turn to me I pray. If you want life you will find it in me alone … none other … no one else. I alone stand supreme with all authority and power and might. I stand supreme in love. I am merciful and mighty: that's what I am. I love you dearly, so come to me.

Self and My Kingdom

My kingdom is not as the governments of this world where man elects you for position because of your strength and ability, or because you fight to make yourself known and heard for ascendancy. In the Kingdom of God the more you fight for yourself and the more you assert yourself in the flesh, the less authority you have and the lower you fall in rank.

I seek after the meek and lowly, not those who are self-confident in their own worth and ability. All men were made in my image and likeness, and all have been given authority to rule. Such is the nature I bestowed upon mankind from the moment I created him. But those that I seek for my kingdom are those whose confidence is in me ... not in themselves. That is why I require that you die.

I require that you die to yourself and your abilities, your accomplishments, your dreams, your desires. I require and demand that nothing of you and yours must take precedence over my will, my purpose, and my plan. I require that nothing in you or of you comes even close to competing with the position I must have in your life, if you truly belong to my Kingdom.

It is the way I function. I always work from nothing. It is in creating beauty from ashes, palaces from hovels, kings from beggars, that I am glorified. It is in creating an orchard from a single seed that lay buried in the ground. It is in creating a king from a young infant lying helpless in his mother's arms. ... even from a tiny, near invisible seed germinated through my desire, my plan and my purpose.

I do not get any pleasure or glory from the greatness of man and his accomplishments. I don't get any glory from the skills of a man's hands or the swiftness of his legs because there is nothing in the flesh that can glorify me. It is all passing – transitory and of no value, unless in it you acknowledge me. That is why the magnificent structures over which you stand in awe mean nothing to me, unless in them, you see my glory. That is what you were meant to do and be – to reflect my glory. And without your acknowledgement of me and who I am, then your work is empty and meaningless in my sight.

Go back and look at all the great artists, architects, scholars and creators of the past. See if it was not through me that they gave birth to their great accomplishments. See if it was not through me that ideas came to life and bore fruit. I am the source of all creativity: it is through me that all things come to life. So I designed it, and so it must be. There can be no other pattern for greatness. Any other greatness is not of me, and must and will come to nothing.

I will not, I shall not share my glory with another. There is nothing of my creation that is worthy of my honor save my only begotten, the one in whom I dwelt when he was on earth. The one who was completely united with me in heart and mind, and whose sole purpose and avowed intent was to do my will and walk in my ways.

Do not be fooled. There is none other of my creation whose heart was turned fully towards me like Jesus. In him I placed the fullness of my Spirit, and in him I placed eternal life. He embodies all truth that ever existed, and to him I have bequeathed all my possessions. In him is the hope of mankind, and all the ages. There is no life outside of him. That is why without him you will die eternally – your spirit will die being eternally separated from its source of life. He was given life twice over. He was born the first of my works before the beginning of the ages, and he was crucified in the flesh and rose again with a new body which will never die. That is the life that I offer to all who belong to my kingdom.

And so, all who would seek to belong to my kingdom must imitate my Son ... the joy of my life. You too must die to the desires of the flesh, to the deceitful pleasures of the world, and to the pursuit of mammon. You must die to the pursuit of all these things, and when you have buried them and they are no longer the essence of your very existence, I will be able to bless you abundantly, that you may bask in my glory and give me back glory in return. Then you will know that all things are of me, through me, and from me, and you will not look anywhere else to meet your needs. You will look to me alone, and in that I am glorified.

I promise you life and joy ... the fullness of life that you can never know outside of me. It is a fullness that satisfies every part of your being. That is the fullness of life that I want for my own, and that I have in my hands to give you, if you will seek me with all your heart.

My Word is Life

My kingdom is not meat or drink, the meat or drink that your physical body craves after to stay alive. I should become your meat and drink. Seeking after me should become your life's purpose and goal. It is my word that sustains you, that gives you life, that resuscitates you when you are sick and strengthens you when you are weak, that gives understanding to your mind, and life and flesh to your bones. Pursuit of my word, an ardent desire to follow me and please me, and a hunger and thirst for righteousness will bequeath to you righteousness, peace and joy in the Holy Ghost.

My word is what upholds my kingdom. My word is what gives you life and breath. Your pursuit of my word demonstrates to me that I am truly your king, that I am foremost in your life.

I don't want you to peruse and study and go over only those words that seem to satisfy your physical being. When you do that you are not truly pursuing me, but rather you are pursuing the things that please and interest you. Then, you are not after my heart because your heart is not pure. Then, you are merely seeking your own wishes, desires and dreams. What I want of you is that you seek me in my fullness, in all my righteousness. Then, I know that you love me, and desire me because of who I am. Then, is your heart pure in my sight, and I will show you my face and my favor.

It is all of my word that becomes me. I am all that I speak. So you have to see me in all that I say, to know who I truly am. Not to do that is to reject me. You cannot accept my word partially, or accept only a part of me. I encompass all my words. It is in them that you have life, that you get wisdom and understanding. It is in them that you find yourself and are fulfilled.

My words, however, cannot be grasped with the human understanding. It is the spirit that I place within you which listens to my own Spirit, and is able to reveal the truth of my words to you. Then and only then can you know me. That is the only way you can understand my heart, and love me with the perfect love that I require of you.

If you can understand the words or the message in the wind that blows, then you can understand my words with your own intellect and wisdom. Then you can understand my language without the interpretation of my Holy Spirit. But you cannot. I have not given it to you to understand my words outside of my Holy Spirit. My words are pure, absolutely pure, without any fault or malice. My words are like light. They are simple and clear to the discerning … the discerning who know and understand that it is only through my Spirit that they can be broken and eaten as food.

Like me, there is no darkness in my words at all … no duplicity no pretense. They are truth and they are life in the same way that my Son – my only begotten Son who I sent to you, is truth and life. Anything that goes against my word is a lie … anything … anything, no matter how real or how genuine it seems to your senses. Everything is a lie that does not conform to my word. My word comes from my heart and depicts who I am. I give my word for life – to create life and the things that please me. So study my word to find me and to know my heart and the things that interest me. Study it diligently and carefully to find my heart.

I want you to know me, to find out things about me, that you cannot even dream of. I want to reveal myself to you, intimately. But I need you to be focused, to pay attention to me closely – to all that I have to say – not just some. I am your joy and your great delight. In me you will find the fulfillment for which you search.

I mean all of my words – I mean all that I say. I was not prompted to say them by anyone. I choose what I say, when I say, and to whom I say. It is up to you to believe or not to believe what I tell you. I cannot lie; it is impossible for me to lie. There is nothing about me that can be a lie or tolerate lies. Even if the thing were not so before, if I say it, and once I say it, it becomes truth. I am truth, the essence of truth. The word *truth* simply means *my word* because that is the only thing that cannot change, and truth never changes. That is the origin of truth … my word … that which never changes. From that you have interpreted it to mean other things.

I tell you again, it is impossible for me to lie. If the thing that I say to you does not come to pass, it is because you have not kept my word wholly – totally. Because my word is truth, if I lay down a condition for a thing to be, then the condition must be met before the thing can come to pass. It just has to be that way. If it were not so, then I would become a liar. My word would not be true: I would become false. And it is impossible for that to happen.

No Delight ...

I love you, my creation, and I want your joy to be full. I take no delight in your pain and sorrow. I take no pleasure in it ... no joy at all. Nor do I delight in the death of the wicked. I am God, pure and holy. I cannot be anything less than what I am, pure and holy and true.

I want you to understand me and know me more. My heart goes out after you in love and compassion. I share your pain and your grief. I never laugh at you or mock you. I do not scorn you, for you are my own. How could I laugh at the pain of those who are meant to bring me joy and delight? Or whose sacrifice I look to as a pleasing incense in my nostrils?

I do hurt with you and for you, even though you don't know or understand, or will not believe. My heart aches with longing for your obedience and ensuing joy. I delight in your joy and laugh at your pleasures. You, with my Son, are my delight. Read my word and see me in it. See what I have done, and still do.

I want you to know that I understand that you are flesh ... that you are born with sin and in sin, not by your own choice, but by the choice of your first father. And in my love, I have shown you a way, the only way to overcome the pain and distress of sin.

I did that because I love you and want you to know how much you mean to me.

It is the Devil who is the liar and the one who is deceiving you. He has told you that I scorn you and mock you, and that I do not care for you or the pain and distress that you experience. Why then did I come in the flesh? I knew from before I created you that you would rebel against me, but in spite of that, I chose to make you into my own image and likeness. I loved you before I made you, even when I knew you were going to reject me and break my heart. But I decided that I wanted a part of my creation to be like me. I wanted to see you demonstrate and reflect my glory on the earth in which I placed you.

I tell you, even before I made you I knew what you were going to do, so I determined in my own heart, from the beginning, that I would give up my glory and come down to earth myself in the form of a man, to experience your life in the flesh and the temptations of sin; to understand all that you go through; and then die for you so that you can all attain to the position I originally designed for you.

So how could I not love you and care for you? I am the branch from which you came and the root from which you sprung.

Family Tree

If I didn't love you and want to identify myself with you, I would not have come through a line of people like Judah, your depraved father, and his malicious daughter-in-law; through Rahab, the prostitute; Ruth, the Moabitess, or David, the murderer and adulterer. I could have created a pure and sinless line of people and set them apart from all human kind. But I chose to come through a line that demonstrated the weaknesses and strengths of the race of people I created.

I wanted to show through my servants, Abraham and David, what you are capable of achieving and becoming when you trust in me. But I also wanted to show you that I understand the human limitations under which you operate. Through my servant David, I wanted you to know that I do not abandon you when you fall into sin. Like a father, I will chastise you, but if you acknowledge and embrace my chastening, repent and turn to me, I will forgive you of your rebellion, and embrace you in my bosom once more.

Even when I cause you to be devastated, and scatter you from the land I give to you, if you turn your heart towards me, and follow me with everything within you, then even in bondage and in foreign lands, like Daniel and the three Hebrew boys, I will cause you to fare well.

Remember, I am King ... I am King and Lord over all the universe, over all creation, and none ... no one, none of my creation can thwart my ways or my purposes. What I will, will come to pass. So even when I allow the enemy to tempt you, the Devil himself has to turn aside and stop when I beckon to him, 'It is enough'. Remember, like my Son, you too will rise again one day in complete victory.

Peace with Persecution

My kingdom is a kingdom of peace. I do not delight in the death of the wicked; I do not delight in fights and wars. Wars exist to destroy the work of the enemy, not to destroy mankind. But if man chooses to give his life and spirit over to the enemy, then he too will be destroyed along with the works of darkness, which he perpetuates. But even war does not destroy the peace of my kingdom.

The peace that permeates my kingdom is the heart peace that results from union between me and my creation. It is a peace that can only be experienced when you understand and embrace my perfect love: it comes when you trust me with all your heart. Then you live in that state of being which reassures you that whatever I say or do is out of love for you. When you get to that place in your heart, then you will begin to experience the real peace that pervades my kingdom ... man, animal and nature. There will be total harmony as everyone and everything will know me and its place.

Even now, in your life, when there are wars and disasters around you, you don't have to worry, if you trust in me implicitly, and have my peace in your heart because I promise to protect you and look after you. I promise you that no evil will befall you: I promise that I will give my angels charge over you to protect you lest you dash your foot against a stone.

However, I warn you that you will be persecuted for my name's sake. But that should not take away your peace. Persecution will continue until the day my kingdom fully arrives on earth. But I want you to know that even though you suffer for the sake of my kingdom, it should not rob you of your peace.

Remember, I gave my Son to die for you. He, my son is the Prince of Peace, and yet he was spat upon and beaten beyond recognition. He was nailed on the cross to die a shameful death. He was verbally accused. They called my Son Beelzebub – a devil – yet he was, and still is the Prince of Peace. He experienced grief to the extent that his sorrow literally fell from his face like drops of blood. Even then, he was the Prince of Peace. Even then, he had peace because he was still obedient to my will. All his thoughts and imaginations were in perfect harmony with mine.

That is why the thing that caused him the greatest suffering and agony was not the physical pain of death, but knowing it meant that he would be separated from me for a few moments of time.

For him to die, he had to take sin and rebellion on to himself, and just for that moment … the moment of his death on the cross … my Son understood what it was not to have peace. He experienced torment. Although he didn't take the sin inside of him, it was laid on his body. And so, even though he was my only begotten, dearly beloved Son, I had to turn my back on him because it is impossible for my holiness to remain in the presence of sin.

It was for those three hours on the cross, when all of the sins of the world were placed on him, that peace departed from him so earth could once again experience peace. At that time, the whole creation, the heavens and the earth, shook in anguish and consternation, because I God, had taken sin on myself through my Son so that I could restore real peace to my children … those I created in my own image and likeness, but who in rebellion, had taken it upon themselves to turn away from me, their source of peace and life.

But from the moment he gave up his spirit – the moment that he died – peace was restored to him. So he could now go down to the deepest parts and take back from Satan the keys of death and hell, and restore peace to mankind, even in the grave, because the deed was done. So when he rose from the grave and breathed on his disciples and gave them his peace, it was the peace of perfect restoration and union with me. And even though John was exiled to Patmos, Peter was crucified, Paul was stoned and beaten many times, and the church was scattered and still suffers persecution, you will still have peace if you remain in me.

For mankind, the word peace means the absence of conflict among each other. But that is not what peace is. If external conflict robs you of peace, then you have no peace at all. Peace cannot be so fragile.

Because the earth reels in rebellion against me, there will always be wars and conflicts and disaster in nature. But no matter what happens around you, it cannot shake the inner peace that comes with knowing me.

The peace that I give to you, does not simply come *from* knowing me. It is *knowing me*. Peace is returning to the source from which you came so there is no longer any dichotomy within you. Peace is unity and wholeness, the wholeness that comes from your union with me, which makes us one. That is what peace is for you.

Your lack of peace, which results from your separation from me, is often manifested in quarrels and fights. But it is not the quarrels and fights which signify there is no peace. It is because you have lost your peace why there are quarrels and fights and wars.

When you possess peace – when you are one with me - you can deal with anything that comes your way. Because I am with you, you have nothing to worry about. When your Father and your King is on your side, nothing can touch you unless he allows it to, or no harm will befall you. To remain in my peace you must trust me. I am not speaking about being born again. I mean you must walk with me daily … all the time … whatever you do, wherever you go.

You have to change your perception and understanding of life – turn away from the way the world taught you, to my way. The world judges actions but I judge the heart. So, even though I have given you my peace you can only experience it by abiding in me all the time. That means your heart must be turned fully towards me in trust and confidence, and you must seek to please me in everything you do and say. It is only when you have that complete trust and confidence in me that you experience peace at all times, in every situation.

A Nurturing Kingdom

My kingdom is a nurturing kingdom. I restore the dead to life and comfort the weak and broken. I fill the need for love and compassion and open wide doors for you to realize the creative visions I place within you. Whatever it is you desire on earth or in heaven, my kingdom can meet those needs if you stand upon my word.

I am the author of the dreams and visions that are hidden deep within you. I placed them there within you when you were still unborn and hidden in the deep recesses of the earth. I chose you to fulfill the purpose I designed for you before the foundation of the world. I had it all planned out ages before you were even conceived in your mother's womb. So far back has been my purpose for you within my kingdom.

My kingdom is like a giant garden laden with plants of every hue, shape and size. There are flowers of spectacular beauty, flowers laden with nectar to feed the bees, flowers with stark beauty reflecting strength and resilience, just as there are trees of every stature and purpose under heaven. And I have created them all – everyone with beauty.

In the same way, I have created each of you with beauty and purpose, a purpose which can only be fully attained when you tap deeply into my resources. I want you – all that is within you – your heart, your mind, your spirit. All that I have placed within you, I want it all to be laid on my altar. Then I will take them up again and make them new. I will give them spiritual life, and give them back to you so that you will find your rightful place in life. After I give them back to you then you must do whatever I tell you to do, and say the things I speak to you. You must then take up your position in life with humility. Then, everything spoken into your life will come to pass. Everything I say of you will come into being because my word is life and truth.

You wonder about the personal words you have heard from me in the past. They are there resident within you, maturing and ready to bear fruit at the right time. They are there in your heart and your spirit germinating and taking root deep within you, so that they will not be shaken during the storm, nor the fruit fall to the ground spoiled and wasted.

Many of my words within you have already withstood the storm and the hail, and the winds and the clouds. They have withstood the battering and have dug deep into the soil of your heart, and are now ready to bear fruit, ripe, rich fruit which will spring up untended and unwatched. They will come to life from the soil of your heart which has germinated it.

The fruit, that same fruit, which you know is within your bowels, when plucked will feed your world with its rich nectar. It will be life-giving sustenance to those who eat from it. Although it lies within you, it is not from you: it is only of you, of the things I placed within you, and the situations I sent to fashion and form you. Now it is full grown and ready to come into being.

Just watch and see what happens. Just watch and see how I will bless you, and others through the gifts I have placed within you. Just watch, sit and watch.

I am the mighty God who is in charge, and I have seen your tears … all of you. None has fallen to the ground unattended. I have watched over them and watered them to bear the rich fruit

I require of them, and which I alone can cause to come forth. I am the fruit-bearer, the multiplier, the power, the shedder and the life giver.

I see your desires from the beginning, even during your youth. I see your needs and your heart's bent, and I let you so that you can know yourself, then turn to me and trust me only. For your dream can only be fulfilled in me alone. I am your own. So now just rest in me; lean on me; have faith in me. I am the answer to all your questions, hopes, desires and dreams. When I am in you and you are in me, we become one, and I will bless you, even as I will be blessed. I want you just to trust in me. Don't worry; don't cry or fret. Just trust in me alone. I am your hope and answer to life. I am the fruit bearer, not you. Just bless me, and give thanks as I bring you gifts and your dreams to fruition.

No Midway

I am my kingdom, and my kingdom is me. In truth, I am the embodiment of my kingdom. You cannot seek for my kingdom without seeking for me or knowing me because I am central to the kingdom. I am the central force behind the kingdom. Without me there is no kingdom, and there is no kingdom without me.

Thus, to speak of my kingdom without knowing me personally is a travesty. It cannot be done. Without a king, there is no kingdom: there is no law or constitution or culture. The king is the life of the kingdom; he owns everything in his kingdom. Kingdom is simply the word used to describe a king's possession. Whatever is in one's kingdom belongs to him.

So, it is with my kingdom. I am Lord over all. There is nothing in my kingdom that I do not own: there is nothing that I do not know: there is nothing that is hidden from me in my kingdom. I know all about you because you are mine, I know where you reside, I know your friends, I know your thoughts and desires; I know your every wish and your very imagination. There is nothing unknown to me, not even the secret thoughts buried deep down inside of you, which you have not admitted, even to yourself.

There is nothing that can be concealed from me because I, your King, am the all knowing God. I am the omnipotent and the all wise God. I knew you before you were born – I know the very circumstance of your birth to the last details. I alone can give life, and if I give you life, I have a good purpose for your life. So, if you trust me and walk in my way, there is nothing that will happen to you by chance.

But it is only in knowing me, trusting me, and walking close to me that the good purposes of your life will be fulfilled.

Remember that the enemy also has a design on your life. He too has a plan laid out to bring you to ruin because that is his sole aim and purpose. He is the master of destruction, and his life's mission is to steal, kill and destroy. But he is a wily creature, the most cunning and subtle of my creation, and he will make you think what he is doing is good for you. He will make it seem like his way, or what *you* think is your own way, will make you prosper. But it is a deception. His goal is to destroy you and rob you of the blessings and the gifts I send into your life.

And you can, and will be easily deceived by his cunning, if you don't tap into my eternal wisdom. He will lead you into the path of evil and make you seem to thrive. But believe me, when I, who see and know all things, tell you that outside of me, the end is death.

If you trust in me, I will work all things for good, even the vile and wicked schemes of the enemy. But, I won't intrude in your life. I have laid bare the paths before you: I have placed openly before you the choices you can make. I am a just and righteous God, so I withhold nothing from you. I tell you plainly what is the end of the road for the two choices open to you: if you turn away from me, and allow yourself to be deceived by the enemy, the end is death and destruction. If you turn to me and listen to me, and conform to my teaching, then the end is life and peace and blessing.

I am telling you plainly, there is no midway in life. There are only two paths you can take … the way of life in my kingdom, and the way of death in Satan's kingdom. There are only two spiritual kingdoms, and everyone of the race into which I breathed my own breath at creation, belongs to one or other of these two kingdoms. Ignorance is no excuse because I have told you.

Even if you think you are independent, and that you are simply doing things your own way, then you are in rebellion against my word, and have chosen the kingdom of darkness. If you don't listen to my words, and if you don't follow my instructions or my counsel, then you belong to the kingdom of darkness.

I have told you, and I am telling you again, you cannot be neutral. You are the race I have chosen to make in my own image and likeness, and have appointed you as stewards of the earth to demonstrate my glory. It is for that reason that I gave you life. However you must understand that for your stewardship to be successful, it must be carried out according to my instruction and design. It cannot be done half-heartedly, partially or imperfectly. For your work to be successful, it must be executed in full conformity with my instructions.

I am the one who places vision and purpose within you. And I am the one who will instill in you the creative steps to fulfill the vision I have given to you. I am your source of life, and in following me lies the fulfillment of your dreams and visions. But you must listen to me keenly, and follow closely everything I tell you. Do not deviate to the right or to the left. I am a God of details, who sees all things … past present and future. And I have all things measured out in time. Therefore, you must pay attention to all I say. Everything I say, not just some things.

I must tell you that the best way to hear me is to spend time with me alone. Spend lots of time in my presence, away from the hustle and bustle of life around you. Find your own place of quiet like my servant, David, as a young boy out in the fields watching over his father's sheep – and let our hearts become entwined. Just calm yourself and put away all thought of the worries of life, and listen to me. Listen to what I say in your spirit, directly from my heart to yours. Listen to what I am saying in the trees and flowers, and mountains around you. Listen to what I am saying through the skill of the musician, the artist, the painter or architect in the man-made designs around you. See me in all things beautiful, even the wisdom of the animals and the miraculous way I watch over them in the wild and feed them. Just see my glory all around you.

But do not be deceived. Many will try to rob me of my glory, and refuse to acknowledge me for the gifts and talents and abilities I have placed within them. Be alert, and recognize those who would seem to take my glory for themselves, and turn away from their ways. I am the creator of all things beautiful. Don't forget it is the enemy who has perverted man to mar the beauty which lay inherent in all created things and to abuse the purposes of my design. But you, of my kingdom, must not be caught among those who pervert and destroy.

Two Kingdoms

If you belong to my kingdom, you have to separate yourself from the kingdom of darkness. The two kingdoms cannot co-exist in one place or in one body. Either your body and your whole being belong to me, or you belong to the other kingdom. I say there can be no dichotomy: you cannot serve two masters. You will 'hate the one and love the other', or 'be devoted to the one and despise the other' (Matthew 6:24).

One of the hallmarks of my kingdom is holiness, which is wholeness. Either you belong fully to my kingdom, or you don't. You do not belong even if you are standing just right outside the gate. Even if you are one toe outside the door, you are still out. You have to resolve with your whole heart to come in. Then you are mine, and I will begin to teach you and show you the treasures of my kingdom. But you must make the decision to step in, and turn your heart towards me fully. That is all you need to do, and my Spirit will guide you the rest of the way.

Standing just outside the door or the window and looking in and vicariously delighting yourself in the joys and pleasures that the people in my kingdom enjoy, is of no value to you, unless it entices you to come in yourself. I am the only one who should stand at the door – I am the door, and I stay wide open waiting for you to enter and share my life.

Full Obedience

Only what exists in heaven, in the spiritual realm is real. There lies the original, I designed for life on earth. That which is on earth, which you see with the natural eye is not real, since it is passing. It is only transitory. That is why when I give you instructions and I tell you specific details of what to do and how to act, it is because I am preparing you for the real life, the life that is eternal.

Thus, you cannot disobey me or obey me partially, and expect to have my pleasure. Total disobedience, or partial obedience means you have defied my word, and that means what you have done does not conform to the measurement of the blue print that exists in the spiritual realm. It is therefore repugnant to me: it is unacceptable to me since it does not conform to my design. And you cannot be rewarded for disobedience.

You do not understand the far reaching nature of disobedience. Disobedience results in the destruction and dismantling of structures, ideas and designs which have been established from the beginning of time in the spiritual realm and in my mind.

I am the original designer and creator of all things, and I do all things well. There is no evil in me. I am God and I am good: I am the essence of goodness and truth. I am truth itself.

So whatever does not conform fully to my word is a lie. Believing a half truth is believing a lie, and Satan is the father of lies. I cannot lie. Truth is whole and complete. There can be no gaps or inconsistencies. Then it is not truth.

In my kingdom you must learn to obey me fully, and act in accordance with all I tell you. You cannot pick and choose what to do. That is why I say, if you do not understand my word, come to me, and my Holy Spirit will make it plain to you. I tell you if you lack wisdom, you should come to me, and I will give you liberally of my wisdom without chiding you.

That is why I tell you to seek wisdom and understanding above all things – to seek it with all your heart. You are to seek it as if your last breath depends upon it. Wisdom is at the street corner and on the mountain tops. Wherever you go, I have sent wisdom calling out to you to get your attention. She is everywhere, but she will never force herself upon you. So although she is everywhere – just at your beckoning – you cannot see her until you set your face to seek for her. But beware! The woman, Folly is also everywhere. She is an imitation, and wherever wisdom goes, there she is calling out as loudly to whoever will listen. She is easy to follow because she does not demand commitment, and she pleases the flesh.

She, Folly is easy to follow because she is a liar who withholds the truth. She keeps from you the depths of her deception; she covers over the tragic pain and loss you will experience when you go her way. Deception and insincerity is her game. So I warn you, do not follow her. Her end is destruction.

The pleasure she gives to you is only temporary – very short-lived. The fame and renown she gives to you will soon disappear. She will seem to exalt you and make you feel great, but she will turn around the next minute and expose your weaknesses and mock you. The same world that she caused to praise you, and exalt you while you thought she had securely ensconced you above all those around you – it is the same world, the same people whom she will cause to expose you, tear you down, and destroy you.

Those who once praised you will now mock you and scorn you. Folly herself will laugh at you in the end. However, even at that point, if you turn to me, and repent of your waywardness, I will forgive you. I will wash from you the dirt and the stain which folly and the world plastered all over you. I will clean you up so that you can begin a new life. But you must follow Wisdom wholeheartedly. Follow all her instructions, then she will exalt you. Humble yourself and seek healing and redemption and she will save you.

However, my kingdom is built on truth, so I cannot deceive you that there will only be success, merriment, laughter and prosperity in my kingdom on earth. There is success and there is merriment, and there is laughter, but I am a God of vision and purpose. I am a hardworking God who knows what needs to be accomplished, by whom, and when. My eyes rove over the earth at all times. I go up and down the earth to do good on behalf of those who love me.

I engrave on the palm of my hands all you, who belong to my kingdom. I watch over you carefully to see that your life conforms to the image in which I made you … to ensure that you fulfill all the plans and purposes I designed for you, and to ensure that you take time to tap into my resources … that you tap deep into your own soul and spirit to find the vision I implanted inside you at birth.

Many of you live without finding it, and my heart is grieved. I hurt to see the waste of the resources and talents I have placed within you. So, don't grow weary or frustrated, and think I do not love you, or that I have forgotten you, when I test and try you, and do everything I can to get you on the path I designed for you. Sometimes I have to wake you and shake you, and pull the rug out from under your feet just to get your attention.

It will cause you pain and discomfort, and you might think I am a hard and cruel God when I allow you to go through the hardship and pain necessary to wake you and get you on the path of your purpose. Some of you get stiff-necked and complain. You turn your back on me because you think the agony I allow you to go through is too severe – too unbearable. Your problem is that when you are going through the pangs you often forget my promise that I will not allow you to go through more than you can bear. You momentarily forget that I am a God of my word – that I am a God who cannot lie and who cannot forget. You forget that I am a God of purpose – and that if you belong to me and are walking in my word, everything I permit in your life is for the fulfillment of my purpose.

My purpose is supreme. I am *El Shaddai*; I am *Alpha and Omega,* the beginning and the ending, the first and the last. I am the designer of life and time, and I know all things and see all things at a glance. I am in control of all situations and all of life, and nothing can happen outside of my knowledge. So because I see and know all that is, and because I love you, you must trust me regardless of how things might seem to you. If I am your Lord and king, then you must trust me, even in the pain.

Remember that because of my love for you, I put my own Son through the most heartbreaking and unbearable pain there is – betrayal and death by the people you love, for the people you love. His pain wasn't just in dying for you, but the greater pain was in his separation from me. He was an obedient and perfect Son who possessed not even the slightest trace of rebellion against his Father. There was perfect unity between us. He always sought to do my will and he had his Father's heart of love and compassion. He was equal to me and there was no stain or sin found in him at all. Yet, because of love, he suffered the ultimate separation from me – death. And he carried all the sins of the world, the rebellion and evil which he himself detested because he was altogether righteous and holy.

So he bore the spiritual pain of sin in his body, and suffered the physical pain of beating and thorns and nails, and he suffered the shame and mockery of death on a cross. It was hard, but it was for a purpose – the only purpose that really matters – the purpose that serves an eternal end.

Remember ... don't ever forget that this life is transitory. Only the life that is of my kingdom is eternal. Thus the ultimate purpose that I have designed for you on earth, is to determine your place in my kingdom when it fully arrives.

So, if I take you through tests to equip you for your ultimate role in my kingdom, it is because those tests bring out those qualities and gifts I have placed within you that are required for your fulfillment. You must persevere ... keep on going. Don't give up. In this life, and in the life to come, you will be rewarded.

The Eagle

My kingdom is a shelter that the eagle provides for its young. Like the eagle, I nurture you and teach you how to fly. I instruct you in the rudiments of life and everyday living, and teach you how to deal with distractions and challenges that come your way. I feed you and comfort you and I gently lead and guide you until you can understand what life is about … and live.

I tend you like how the eagle nurses its young. I feed you with my own mouth when you are young and helpless, and keep you from harm and evil. I protect you from the craftiness of the enemy which you are not equipped to deal with as a young babe. I watch over you daily, night and day until you are strong and healthy.

Then I begin to thrust you a little and withhold the tiny morsels from you. Then I take you up in my own arms and carry you to places which might seem high and dangerous, just so you can see and understand a little more of the life I have designed for you.

Then I let you gently fall from the comfort and safety of my arms that you might learn to fly – that you might begin to use the wings which I have equipped you with. That you might understand the power and strength I have placed within you.

But even though I let you fall out of my arms to develop your wings, I swoop down right beneath you to catch you, if, and when your wings are not strong enough to carry you. I never let you fall to the ground. But, if, at times when you should be a mature bird, you let fear and cowardice keep you from flying with your own wings, and you still seem satisfied to depend on me to search for food, and to take it you and feed you with my own mouth, then I will let you fall to the ground. But you will never be destroyed.

Even though you fall to the ground, as long as you respond to me and look to me, I will tend to you and bandage your wounds and bruises and pour oil upon you, and in you to heal you. But, even then, I cannot let you remain on the ground. I love you too much to see you throw away the awesome gifts and the potential I have placed within you.

So, I will take you back up in my arms and let you go again and again, as long as you keep trying, even if you fail over and over and over, a million times over. I will always be there to catch you or mend your broken bones. But in my kingdom, I cannot – will not – let you waste the life I have given you. I must do all in my power to help to strengthen you, to ensure that all the resplendent glory I have placed within you comes to the fore.

As long as you get up with a willingness to try I am there to lift you back up. Even if all you have the strength to demonstrate is a mere lift of the head in hope, then I am there. And even if you don't lift your head, but simply turn your eyes, or twitch your wing or just a feather to respond to me or any other eagle I send in your path, I will respond to you. And I promise I will send many eagles to you.

But, and if you lie there devoid of all hope, and if you turn away from me and those I send in your path to quicken you and nurse you back to life, then you will make yourself die. If you do not turn your head; if you do not slit open your beak to receive the food I send your way, then you will have caused yourself to die.

Then you would have rejected the ultimate gift I have given to you … the gift of hope … which is founded on confidence in who I am and my faithfulness to fulfill the inherent promise you feel inside of you. When you reject that hope, you make me impotent to help you.

I have placed that hope within each of my creation. It was my first gift to you, coming out of my very own being. It is the thing that makes you rise in the morning and go through day after day, year after year, carrying out the routine activities of life. The hope which I have given to every man and woman lies in the knowledge of a good future … eternal life … regardless of the struggles of this present life. That hope was breathed into you when I breathed my own spirit into the first man. It is the gift that holds your life together, and is manifested in your faith in me and my word. It is the one gift without which your physical life cannot be sustained.

Without hope you will die. By your rejection of that gift which is essential to life you will die. But I would not have not killed you. It is not my desire for you to die. I want you to really live though, not just exist. I want you to have abundant life beginning here and now. So do not grow weary and tired with the tests and trials you face. Be like your father Abraham:

> *Against all hope, Abraham in hope believed and so he became the father of many nations just as it had been said to him.* (Romans 4:18a NIV)

A New Heart

Your heart is paramount in my kingdom. It is your heart that determines your character. You are not the sum of your qualifications, interests or accomplishments, nor are you tantamount to whatever fame or notoriety is attached to your name. It is your character that makes you who you are, and that is of inestimable value in my kingdom.

What you think in your heart and your mind determines your character. And it is your heart that I judge because that is the seat of your emotions and the source of how you perceive life. And ultimately, that is what determines all your actions and your decisions. That is why your heart has to be right. That is why I say you need a new heart to come into my kingdom.

The heart you are born with cannot bring you success in my kingdom. You are born with a tainted heart, not because of anything you did, but because of the blood of your first father which runs through your veins. You first father sinned and you are born of his lineage, regardless of where you were born, the color of your skin, the language you speak or the ethnic group from which you derived.

You, to whom I speak, belong to the one race of people who I created, and in whom I breathed my own breath and placed my own spirit. I created one man, and from his blood flows the blood of all mankind who ever lived on this earth. This man sinned and severed the intrinsic connection he had with me. By his rebellion he severed the most vital connection between us – the union between man's spirit and my Holy Spirit. My Spirit is holy and pure and cannot dwell with or in any kind of impurity. So by taking sin onto himself, Adam died spiritually. He broke our unity and that of all mankind with him … when you are separated from me, you are spiritually dead.

So, that's why I tell you that you are born in sin: I know it is difficult for you to grasp, but I am making it clear to you that you are a sinner – you are born in a state of rebellion against me. But I have made a way for you to be reconciled to me, and that is the only way – there is no other way. Because I am a holy and perfect God my laws are immutable, and that is why I myself, had to come down from heaven to restore your relationship with me. It had to be according to my law … according to my word.

It was designed from the beginning that experiencing real meaning in life lay in your connectedness to me and your obedience to my word. That was a natural law I wrote from the beginning, and like all my natural laws, breaking them leads to severe consequences. In this case, the consequence of rebellion was death. Your father died spiritually, and so did you.

I cannot break my law, then I would become dishonest, unethical and without integrity, so I decided on a way to restore you to myself. I came down to earth as a man in the form of my Son, Jesus Christ, and once and for all took the punishment for your sin. I myself went on the cross and shed my own blood so that you can be restored to me. I had to shed my blood because life is in the blood and that was the only just way for justice to be done – blood for blood. Your sin had to be paid for, and since death was the consequence of your sin, I chose to die in your place so that you could return to the life I intended for you from the beginning.

The reason why I myself had to die is that sinful blood could not atone for sinful blood and all mankind has the same blood. But Jesus was pure and holy. Although he was born of a natural woman, his blood did not have human DNA. It was pure blood, not from any man of the human race, so he had no sin. And because of his holiness, he could stand in the gap for those who were born in sin … that is the entire human race.

So now all you have to do to get a new heart and become reconnected to me is to accept what my Son has done for you. Then I will begin to build you, and your values will change and little by little your character will begin to be transformed into the image of my Son who always pleases me.

One Way into My Kingdom

Again, I say, the only way to enter my kingdom is to believe my Son. I sent him to die that you might be reconnected to me … so that my kingdom might reign in your heart, and that you might live forever with me.

I love you. I have told you that over and over again. I want you to understand that that is the basis of all my actions concerning you. I love you with all my heart, but I am also just as holy as I am love. Therefore I cannot tolerate sin, and that is what I want you to understand. So when I allow things to happen to you that seem like I don't love you, know that it comes from who I am.

You have to change to suit me. That is the nature of our relationship. Even though I gave you a mind and creativity and a free will, I am still God. Even though I love you, I am the Father and you are my offspring, and I require obedience of you. Love does not change my laws. Love does not condone unrighteousness, so all that happens around you must be seen in light of not only my love, but also my holiness.

My kingdom is founded on my love and my righteousness, and there can be no conflict between the two. They must go hand in hand. Love without righteousness is promiscuity, and righteousness without love is tyranny.

You must understand that my love is different from all other love because it is based on perfect knowledge. So you can trust my love. I know all that you have ever done, or even thought, or imagined. I know what you are capable of. I know everything in your heart … the doubts, the fears, the evil thoughts ... and I love you just the same. The only thing left for you to perfect that love is for you to believe me.

You must learn to believe me, to trust in me. I know that it is difficult at times. I know because I made you and I know how you think … the direction in which your thoughts go. I even knew you would sin before I made you, but my purpose was, and still is, to create a race of people who will be like me … just like my Son … a people who are meek but strong, and who will be able to withstand the vicissitudes of life. Your first father succumbed to temptation and chose to give in to the enemy. He didn't have to because he was equipped with knowledge and every resource needed to stand up against the enemy. But he voluntarily chose to rebel, to disobey, even though I told him plainly what the price was.

Adam chose to follow a woman rather than to obey me. He knew what he was doing; he understood fully the consequences, but he chose a woman over me. Your mother, Eve was deceived. She chose to follow her emotions, her physical desires, rather than obey me.

It was the sin of Adam that caused the fall of the entire human race. It was the man whom I made the father, and in whose seed dwelt all the generations to come after him. When he chose to honor the woman above me and partake of that fruit, then the race of mankind fell. However, even with his chosen path of rebellion, my purpose still stands. I am God, and all my purposes will stand. Every word that I speak will come to pass.

Did I not say to my Son,

Let us make man in our image, after our likeness:
and let them have Dominion over the fish of the sea,
and over the fowl of the air, and over the cattle, and

> *over all the earth, and over every creeping thing that*
> *creepeth upon the earth.* (Genesis 1:26). *And ye shall*
> *be unto me a kingdom of priests, and an holy nation*
> (Exodus 19:6b).

And everything I say will come to pass. Man, as I created him to be, will have the dominion I have built into him. Because I have said so, it will come to pass. Because *I* have spoken man into my own image and likeness, man *will* be formed into my image and likeness, according to my will. And that is what I am doing with you, when I say I have called you and predestined you to be conformed to the image of my Son.

So whatever I allow to happen to you or allow you to go through, know it is that I am transforming you into his image. He came to live among you and personally teach you the way to live. He had to die so that you don't have to die. But I have designed it that in order for you to reign with him in my eternal kingdom, you have to share his experience – you have to suffer with him.

Because your first father succumbed to the pride of the enemy, you have been infected with that pride that comes from a twisted and rebellious character. And my Son has shown you, that even though he was perfect, the only way to be victorious over that deformity is through test, trial and suffering. It is that which perfects you in the long run: not success or prosperity.

Have I not said that if a grain of wheat falls into the ground and dies, it will bear much fruit and if it does not die it will stand alone?

Death is suffering. To die to oneself causes much pain. My Son had to physically die for you. Your death is death to self. And in the same way that the physical death of my Son came through much pain, rejection and torture, so in a lesser way, you will experience death to self.

I myself suffered the pain and agony of having to turn my back on my Son. To turn my face away from one in whom there was no guile, was the most treacherous thing I have ever done.

If injustice were ever to be named of me, it would be that I sent a just man to his death – an ignominious death – to redeem an unjust people. But he had the same love that I had for you from the beginning, and he himself offered to die in your stead. He had to die to redeem you because I am a holy and just God who keeps his word and sticks to his purpose.

So that is why I allow you to go through pain and suffering and trials at times: it is to strengthen and perfect you so that you can be transformed fully into the image of my Son.

Truth and My Kingdom

I hate pretense. In my kingdom there is no room for falseness or hypocrisy. You must possess truth in the inward parts. Your words must reflect your thoughts and your actions: they must be one. There must be holiness in my kingdom – wholeness of body, mind and spirit.

Nice words, empty words do not appeal to me because I see your heart, and that is what I judge. You cannot impress me because I see the truth; I know the truth; I am the truth. All truth was from me, and is of me. Whatever is not of me – whatever does not come from me – is a lie, no matter how good it sounds.

No matter how much what you see with your natural eyes seems to contradict my word, it is my word which is true and which is real. The problem with what you see and hear is that you often choose to focus on a small portion of my word, and that should not be.

In the same way that your common law defines truth as the whole story, not just a part of it, so is the truth of my word. When you go to court, the law demands truth of you, and makes you swear to tell 'the truth, the whole truth and nothing but the truth.' That means the whole truth with no omissions or additions. So you have to perceive my written word as a whole body of truth that needs to be understood altogether as one. You cannot select parts of my word and separate it from the whole, and consider it truth. My truth must be seen in its entirety.

Kingdom of Mammon or God

Money is the enemy of my kingdom. Money sets itself up as Mammon – a god, and seeks to rob my people of the blessings I have promised them. Money is not the answer to the problem of those of you who are in my kingdom. But rather, putting it in its rightful place will be the answer to many of your problems.

Money is the medium Satan established to seek to control my creation after the fall of man. The enemy has taken all the precious things I have created and placed a monetary value on them, and by so doing has my people worshipping at his feet. My people have been pursuing money when they ought not to, as that is not the answer to their needs. They want to enjoy the things I have created and they think – the Enemy has made them think – that the only way to enjoy my blessing is through the love of money – by having lots of it. But that is not the way I designed it.

The earth and everything in it belongs to me, and I do not need money to give them to you. They are mine and I can give them to you whenever I wish and however I wish. I do not need the Devil's devices to help me. Just come to me and I will give it to you. All I require of you is steadfastness to my word. My word must be hidden deep in your heart, and you must live according to them – all of my words. If you choose to follow all of my words, then that means you love me with all of your heart, and that I am first in your life – first above your own desires, above your family, above your friends, above all that you want and pursue, I must be Number One.

You must pursue my kingdom and my righteousness as utmost priority, so I will be able to give to you all the things that you need, and even more. Just trust me. That is how I expect you to operate in my kingdom – trust me to provide all of your needs – not just some – not just what is left over after you have bowed to the demands of Mammon. Put me before Mammon and see what will happen in your life. I will bless you and give to you far, far beyond your imagination. Through Malachi, I invited you to test me, and I am inviting you to test me now.

Prove me whether I am really King in my Kingdom, and not money. Prove me and see whether I provide for my own, or whether Mammon does. Come and test me; come and prove me. I long to show myself strong on your behalf. I long for you to turn to me and depend upon me fully, completely, totally. I desire… I long to prove myself to you … to show you myself … to show what I can do for you … to show how much I love you and care for you.

I want you to give me the opportunity to bless you, to bless you abundantly beyond your imagination. That is the only way you will be truly blessed, and that is the only way I can truly delight in you, when you allow me to be truly God and King of your life.

I challenge you … turn your back on Mammon, stop worshipping at its feet and turn to me and see what I can and will do for you.

Faith and My Kingdom

Above all, there is one thing you need in order to see me work in my Kingdom, to see all the great and awesome things I would like to do for you. And that is faith. Without faith, I cannot work and you cannot see me work. It is just like that. You have to believe in me, and in what I say in order for me to act – to really work on your behalf.

My hands are tied in the absence of faith. In spite of my great power and might, I can do nothing for you without your using the measure of faith I have placed within you. I have so designed it from the beginning. It is a law I put in place from creation, and it will not change. Neither I, nor my law, can or will change.

Your faith is an intrinsic part of you. It is fundamental to what makes you a human being – as fundamental as the intellect I placed within you – as fundamental as your ability to create and to think. Without faith you can do nothing: nor can I. You were made in my image. I am intrinsically a God of faith, and so are you. I desire, I believe, I speak, and it is done. And it should be so with you. You desire, you believe, you speak, and it is done. This should come from your wholeness of character, from the unity of body, mind and spirit and an internal unity of thought, word and action.

Faith must be firmly grounded for it to be effective. There can be no wavering or vacillation. If there is vacillation, it means there is disunity within you. To achieve that oneness and wholeness within yourself, you must stop trying to control your own life and its circumstances and outcome. Stop thinking that you are ultimately in charge of your own life. Stop thinking that if things don't go the way you want them, you are to blame. Stop carrying the weight of your own life.

I am the one who determines the times and seasons – not you – not the Devil. It is I, your King and your Lord. So you must learn to trust me ... totally. Do what I say, and act when I speak, and then you don't need to worry about anything at all … nothing. I will solve all your problems. Give them to me: I will deal with them. If you have erred, then I require you to repent – confess your sins and repent – and I will forgive you and set you free. You cannot make right what is wrong: I am the only one who can do that. That is why you have to listen and obey me. So confess, repent, stay close to me, and leave it in my hands. That is what I require you to do.

Do that, and then trust me to work out the rest. Remember I am a God who forgives and forgets. Haven't I said I will cast your sins away as far as the east is from the west, and not remember them anymore, if you turn to me? I am a holy God: I mean what I say, and I keep my word. I counsel you to cast all your cares upon me, and I will care for you. I can handle them. I can deal with them. I want to take them and work them out that I might show myself strong on your behalf.

Faith is the source of all of creation and I am the foundation of faith. And I say you have to believe before you can see. Seeing is not believing, as your poets and philosophers have propounded for ages. I say you must believe first, and then you will see. For the things that are important and of lasting and eternal value are first seen in the spiritual realm before they can they can be experienced in the natural. There is a spiritual realm, not visible to the natural eye, but which can only be accessed by faith. So you must believe first, and then you will see. Faith is what places you in right standing with me. When you believe in me the way I require of you, then I will be pleased with you, and you will receive my blessing. Haven't I lifted up before you, the example of my friend, your father Abraham? He believed in me and my word, and thus he was found righteous in my sight.

Faith in My Kingdom

Faith is constant. True faith does not vacillate. If you waver in your life about other decisions, then your faith will waver too. That's why I say you must be consistent in your words and your thoughts. You must be unwavering – a man or woman who keeps your word. Your 'yes' must be 'yes' and your 'no' must be 'no'. And that is why I also require you to be longsuffering. The time will come when you want to change your word because the thing that you pledged to do – the thing that you set your heart to, has become too difficult. But longsuffering means you do it anyway.

You must do it because of faithfulness to my word, not because you want to impress others, or because you are afraid for yourself … afraid of change … of the future … of how others will look at you, or what they will say about you. But you must stick to it because of your faithfulness to me. Then I will reward you; then I will work for you, and show myself strong on your behalf. I tell you I am no man's debtor. If you suffer on my behalf, in strict obedience to my word, then I will reward you. You will be duly recompensed, both here and in the life to come.

But you must keep in mind that it is the heart I judge, not the action. So, don't be deceived when all men praise you because of what you do, and how laudable and praiseworthy your actions seem to them. Man does not, or cannot judge the heart. That is my job; that is why the judgment of man is worthless. It is hollow and carries no weight in my kingdom.

The spirit of longsuffering that I require you to develop is similar to that which my Son learned while he was on earth. He knew that he came down to earth for a reaSon, and he had to endure whatever it took to accomplish that purpose. Just that last day on earth as a man – those few hours before he renounced his life on the cross, truly taught him what obedience and longsuffering meant.

The physical pain and insults were unbearable when they mocked him as he fell beneath the weight of the cross more than once. But he had to rise up and walk again because he had committed himself to dying for mankind: that is the epitome of what longsuffering is. It literally means 'to suffer long'. Of no other man, have I required what I required of my Son. Yet, I expect you to share in his suffering since you will share in his glory.

Longsuffering is a part of my own nature. Don't you know it is a part of the fruit of my own Spirit? That is why you, as a people have not been consumed by my wrath. It is because of my faithfulness and my longsuffering.

And you are mine – my very own – you were made in my image and likeness, and I expect you to reflect my very heart and nature. So strengthen yourself in me. Determine in your heart to be as I am, and you will never be put to shame. I myself will honor you and reward you. What you deprive yourself of might seem small to you and to others, but I count it of value and inestimable worth to me when you make a sacrifice on my behalf. I will honor you for it. Just look to me and see if I will not be faithful to my word.

My faith and faithfulness are two sides of the same coin. Faith demands faithfulness. You must be faithful to the word that I speak to you. And in your faithfulness do you demonstrate faith in me. Both words come from the same root, but faithfulness is a precursor to the development of faith – the great faith that I require of you in order that I might show greatness through you.

It works like this. The seed of faith that I have planted in your very genes generates in you a desire to know me and to follow me. Once you respond to the instinct of that faith that I placed within you, your faithfulness develops. As a consequence, the more you are faithful to my word, the more you know me, and grow to trust me, and in me – who I am, and what I say. That is faith.

Love and Justice

I am a God of integrity, and the tenets of my kingdom are righteousness, justice and love. The way I treat you is the proof of my own integrity, and my integrity is reflected in the constancy of my word.

I created you in love, and my sense of justice and righteousness are reflected in the way I deal with you ... you who belong to me ... you who are of my own blood ... you who belong to my kingdom, and for whose welfare I am responsible. And that is how I invite you to see me and judge me, whether I am a God of righteousness, justice and love. However, you cannot judge me by standards which you have set for yourselves because your standards are based on your own selfishness and self-centeredness. Your standards are based on your physical senses and experience, and your partial knowledge.

You have to judge me based on my standards, by my holiness, by what I say about myself, by what I do, and by the faithfulness of my word. Because I possess perfect knowledge and perfect understanding of all things, for your judgment of me to be valid, it must be based on your perSonal knowledge of me. And you can only know me by spending time with me so you can become acquainted with my thoughts and get to know my heart.

In truth, any judgment – yours or mine – can only be just to the extent that it is based upon an intimate knowledge of the thing or person that you judge. So when I invite to judge me, I am also demanding obedience and expecting intimacy from you. Only then will my Holy Spirit be able to reveal to you the truths hidden in what I say, so that you can understand the real meaning of all things that I utter.

Without the Holy Spirit, you cannot know me. He is the only one who has been given the authority to reveal the truth of my words to you. He is the only one who knows and fully understands all that I say. In the same way when Jesus was on earth, he spoke in parables to the crowds, but only revealed the secret of his truth to those who were committed to following him, so it is today.

Even though my words are written in a book, they cannot be grasped by the natural mind. Only my Holy Spirit can give a true understanding of what is written there. That is why I say my words are like silver tested in the fire seven times. They are pure. My words are clear and transparent, pure and malleable to those who hear through the Holy Spirit. They are malleable in that they can be molded to suit your situation, but they never change. The true meaning and essence of my words remain fixed, but the application depends on the situation.

When I tell you that I am your shepherd and you will not want, it means that you will not want for bread. It means that you will not want for my daily spiritual food in your life. It means you will not want for an answer or solution when you are in trouble. It means you will not want for a place to lay your head, when you need it. It means you will not want when you hunger and thirst after righteousness, when you trust in me. It means that you will not want for comfort when you are sad. It means that you will not want for anything you are in need of when you allow me to shepherd you. My Holy Spirit will reveal to you through your own desire, the nature of the sheep who never wants.

My word contains no dross or impurity. There is no duplicity, no contradiction for those who seek the truth because my Holy

Spirit is the spirit of truth. Whatever he reveals to you of my word is the truth for your circumstance and situation. I do not speak to any man or woman except through my Holy Spirit. Without my Holy Spirit, no one can say "God said" or "God told me". All else is a lie. Whatever does not conform to, or concur with what my Spirit says, is of another spirit, and is not the truth.

My Spirit only speaks what the Word tells him. He cannot speak of his own. Jesus is the living Word, and every word spoken by the Holy Spirit will honor Jesus for who he is. Jesus on the cross was the ultimate test of my love for you and the purity of my word. I had to show you what real love is. He is the symbol of my love and my word.

Even so, your love for me and my word in you must be tested. You are like me. I made you in my own image and likeness, so I treat you the way I treat myself. Whatever I or my word says you are, that is exactly what you are, and I don't allow you to go through anything that you cannot deal with. I have told you so and I mean it: I expect holiness and righteousness of you because so I am, and I have placed everything in you and at your disposal, to live and act accordingly.

An Open Door

I am a king with an open door. I invite you to come into my private chamber – into my very throne room to fellowship and dine with me.

I delight in your presence; you are a sweet smelling savor to me, incense that brings pleasure to my senses. My very heart longs for you, and I take pleasure in communing with you. It is joy to me when you to listen to me and when you talk with me. There is great reciprocity in our communion although you may not know it. I get great delight when you set aside an hour for me alone … to spend time with me apart from everyone else and apart from your daily activities. It is a hallowed time for me to be at the focus of your attention. It opens doors for you to receive my blessing, and brings heart peace.

Not only does your communion with me bless you, but it allows me to get to know you – to know your heart and your deep desires. It is during these times that you reveal your innermost thoughts and your being to me. I already know all about you – I already know what you are – even the thoughts and intent of your heart. But when you come to me, and of your own free will pour out yourself to me, it takes our intimacy and your knowledge of me to a greater level. It bonds our hearts together as friends – even lovers.

It is then, when I get to know your heart as a friend that I get to mold you further into my image, into the image of my Son. Yes, I already possess all knowledge of you, but I need the knowledge of you as a friend to work with you and transform you.

These together moments are the most precious times in both our lives – yours and mine. In these together moments, I can get to bless you and release my grace into your circumstances so that you will have more joy, you and I. Those times can do more for you than any other moment in your life because in those times you revere me and listen to me … you give me the honor that I require of you. And when you honor me, my blessing just flows from my hands – my fingertips. They flow gently, gracefully, profusely – at the pace you are able to handle it.

I love when you spend time alone with me, your Father and your King. I love the attention, and you get the blessing, for so I designed it from the beginning. I must be at the center of your world, and you will receive my reward. So let it be in your life.

Real Life

In my kingdom, there is life … life everlasting, life with meaning, life with fulfillment. I am life. Life is through my Son and outside of him there is only existence.

Real life is fulfilling the purpose for which I created you, and outside of my kingdom that is impossible, because as your King, I am your only source. Your sole purpose in life is to please me. You were created to do my will and my pleasure, and my pleasure is that you experience abundant life.

But if you do not do my will, you cannot accomplish my purpose for you because the fulfillment of your purpose is intrinsically bound up in your connection to me. Even the thing I designed you for from the beginning of the age cannot be realized outside of me. So no matter what you accomplish on your own, it is of no lasting value since there is no true fulfillment outside of me.

It is I, myself, who endow you with gifts and talents through my wisdom and knowledge. It is I who place in your heart those deep desires that will lead to the fulfillment of your purpose. It is also I, who create inroads and open doors for you. I also block the alluring paths the enemy sets up as decoys along the way for you. The enemy knows my heart towards you: he knows that I want to bless you, and so out of envy he sets out to destroy you. He has access to me, and I know he is wily and has set himself up to foil my plans. He wants to lead you astray and destroy you: you cannot win against him on your own. That is why you have to trust me. Therein lies your only hope: trust in me your king who knows you and loves you, and who is the only one able to fulfill your life's purpose.

You cannot look at others to determine your success, or compare yourself with them. You can only measure your development and growth against the original design mapped out for your life, and you have to come to me for that. The enemy will try to thwart you and the plans I have for you. He comes to me for information and permission to do you harm. He does this to test you and me ... to see if you are strong enough, and to see if I am able.

Because his time has not yet come, and because he also is my creation, I speak to him and tell him about you and boast about you like I did with my servant, Job. But his access to you and his ability to do you harm is limited. By simply speaking a word, I myself set boundaries beyond which he dare not and cannot venture.

At times, when what he does to you seem unbearable and cruel, and when you blame me, your King, for his works of darkness I understand and I ache for you. In those times I want you to remember that my love for you can never change. I want you to remember my promise to you not to give you more than you can bear. I do not, and cannot go back on my word. My word cannot be made void unless you step outside of its boundaries.

Know that I place my words within boundaries – within borders. I have to do that. If I don't then other people's disaster and blessings not intended for you would come upon you. To keep within the boundary of my word, you must adhere to all that I tell you personally. If you don't, then you make my word become null and void and you leave spaces for the enemy to creep in and do harm to you that I did not permit him to. He can do it because you permit him to.

I Delight in your work

I take delight in my people, in your joys and your daily life. I delight in your pleasures when they are according to my will and design. I smile when you smile and laugh when you laugh. I want you to be happy, but not insensible; to be joyful, but not irreverent; to laugh but not be scornful. I want you to delight in me, and in me see all your joys.

Your creation is my glory. I delight in when you make the most of the things I give to you, and the gifts and talents that I place within you. Through work, you show your love and gratitude to me. It is in your work that you show my glory, and I shine through you.

You think it is only when you are joyful or when you speak the 'right' things that my glory is seen. Yes, I do shine through you when you laugh and when you talk, but talk can be cheap. It can be meaningless if it doesn't come from your heart, or if it is not a precursor to work or action. It is through work that you become fulfilled as a person, that you show yourself most like me and reflect my glory. It is only when you work that I can work through you. If you do not work, then I cannot work: I cannot accomplish my purpose in and through you.

Work is using your hands, your mind, your thoughts, your very being to accomplish and fulfill the desires and dreams that I place within you. Work will bless you and cause you to prosper – not money. Work is the assignment I have given to you – to work in my kingdom – to establish it that I might be glorified.

I Need Your Heart

For you to benefit from my kingdom, I need your heart … all of your heart … your whole heart. I will not accept anything less than complete devotion.

I require all of your heart that I can effectively work through you and that you might know mine. I loved you from the beginning, enough to die for you to redeem you to myself again, after you first rejected me. In turn, I require first love from you. I must be first in your heart. I am your King and your Father and must be your first love.

You must empty yourself before me - totally empty yourself of all of the fears, doubts, secret thoughts, hopes and dreams … everything. You must make yourself totally vulnerable before me, naked and transparent, and then I can clothe you in my righteousness and with my faith.

I will not accept anything between you and me. You cannot allow anything to come between us, or it will jeopardize our relationship and the blessings I want to give to you.

I know and I understand that you will feel weak and helpless when you empty yourself before me. But this is how it was in the beginning and this is how it is meant to be. There should be no darkness in you ... nothing that should make you want to hide yourself from me. You should be before me, naked and helpless and weak because therein lies your strength ... my strength. My strength can only be perfected in and through your weakness. Your dependence should not be on people, or your gifts or talents, or on money. Your dependence should be on me alone.

I must be your strength, your hope and your joy. All these must come through me alone. You must look to me for all that makes your life worthwhile.

I cannot help but bless you when you make yourself empty and vulnerable before me. Then you truly become my child, and I will look after you and care for you. Then, will the enemy be placed under your feet, and you will trample upon every foe that comes your way, and no plan of the enemy will thwart your progress. Then, you will defy every work of darkness. Your foe will scatter before you and no weapon formed against you will prosper. Also I will open doors never before imagined. Then, you will release the pent up showers of blessing that have been waiting to fall upon you to fulfill your desires.

Only then, when you become a child totally dependent upon me, and reliant on me that you will begin to know me in all of my fullness: Then, you will see me work. Remember, I said unless you become like a little child, you shall not enter the Kingdom of God.

So now to see your life change, to see it completely transformed, just trust in me for everything, for all you need. Just trust in me, and leave it all to me. Leave everything to me.

If I Change

I am God and I will not share my glory with anyone. I *cannot* share my glory with another. Then I would no longer be God. If I changed to become what man, my creation wants me to be, then I would no longer be the God who doesn't change. I would become like man … double-minded and unsure of what is right.

If I gave up my glory to share it with man, as man wants me to, then I would become second to man. Then I would have abdicated my throne to my own creation. And although man does not understand, or the natural mind of man cannot grasp it … then, there would be total chaos and confusion … if I change.

If I gave up my position, the earth would return to what it was before I brought order to it for man to inhabit. There would be darkness and confusion. Then all the stars and the planets – the sun and the moon would crumble and fall. There would be nothing to keep them in place or to keep the waters within their boundaries. Without the order that I have brought into being, man, the glory of my creation on earth, would self destruct … if I change.

It is the constancy of my word that keeps the worlds in place. It is the power of my unchanging word that brings order and maintains the seasons of life.

If I change, I would become more vile and evil than man himself because I possess all the knowledge and wisdom that has existed over the ages. I alone possess all the depths of wisdom to understand and perceive the destruction that would result in all of creation, if I, in whom all things dwell and exist, rescinded my power, authority and glory to man.

I own man and all that I have brought into being. And I don't have a struggle with man, but man has a struggle with me because he cannot get me to bend to his own desires and whim and fancy. But he doesn't understand the outcome... if I change.

I can, and I have given man leeway to exercise his mind and his muscles – to exert himself to every end to find himself and to know himself. I have tried to answer his questions. I have given him authority over my creation. I have opened my heart to him to let him understand what is of lasting value and worth. I have humbled myself to show to him what is good and right and acceptable. To make him know the things that will make him prosper and be fulfilled. But still man murmurs, and complains and criticizes me.

I have forgiven him day after day, from age to age. I have shown him mercy and grace in his rebellion against me, and I have kept pursuing him for his own good. At times, he seems to relent, and listen to my voice, but then he devises his own plan in his heart by which he will come to me. He will not pursue me with all his heart – with a pure heart – to learn my ways. He wants *me* to alter my standards – to become unholy and splintered within myself – thus allowing the Evil One to reign.

He refuses to seek to know me as I am, and not as he wants me to be, so he ends up making images of me, or making a religion of me to try to get as much as he can out of me to make his life prosperous and successful. But me, he doesn't care about. He acknowledges me when I can be of service to him, or when I can benefit him.

I cannot change my kingdom to embrace the self-seeking and devious. I cannot change to give up the holiness of my kingdom to please man, even though I love him. Then would unbridled evil reign – the result which the mind cannot conceive of.

Don't they see what self seeking actions have done, even in the lives of those who loved me? My friend, Abraham, lied about his wife, Sarah and could have destroyed an innocent people. He further perverted my plans for a child in his life, the impact of which waywardness persists even today, resulting in so much war, hatred and evil. David, whom I called the man after my own heart, disobeyed my law and walked after the flesh, bringing great pain to himself and his family.

I need man to understand that I know all of his needs. I made him and understand all the components of his life, and all that is necessary for him. I can meet all of his needs, but I cannot change… not even to please the crown of my earthly creation.

If I change, truth would become a thing of the past because I myself am truth. Truth brings stability and confidence, which begets hope. If I change, there would be nothing to believe in, nothing to hold on to – no one to turn to in distress, no hope and no love. I also embody love.

They don't know it, but they don't really want me to change. They would not want to live if I changed. So I, in love and wisdom will remain unchanging and unchangeable knowing that in me only can man fulfill his purpose and find real joy and happiness.

Conversations

I love to speak with you – to spend time with you. It is my delight and joy. I have so much in me to impart to you, to make your life better, and to give you joy and happiness. I love when you come and sit at my table or at my feet and listen to my heart and my plans and design for you and the world in which I place you.

You are my family. That is why I created you in families, that you might become connected to each other as I am connected, or wish to connect to you. I love you, all of you – from the smallest to the greatest – from the youngest to the oldest – I know each of you personally, by name. I want you individually and together to come to me and spend time with me. My heart is full of love for you and expectation for what I want you to accomplish. There is so much I want for you, but it only comes when you also delight in me, and when your heart becomes knitted to mine.

The things that you enjoy – that are dear to your heart – I also enjoy, and that is why you have the desire for those things. It comes from me. You know deep within yourself when the things you desire are not of me, when they are perverse and unholy. You know the things that defile you and make you unclean and dirty. You know them … you also know the things that I despise. Deep down you know the things that are detestable, and from which you should turn away, but you pretend. You act as if you don't know because you choose to be led astray by those around you, by those of influence and those whom you admire, that are not of my kingdom.

I ask of you ... I beg of you, search deep down into your heart, deep down to find the truths that are written there. That is why I say the heart is deceptive and evil. It knows the truth, but chooses to withhold it. It keeps truth hidden from view, and thus you are led into evil. That is why you need to take control of your thoughts and the things that enter your heart. That is why I say you must guard your heart, so that evil thoughts do not enter and corrupt you. Once you allow the evil around you to enter your heart, it is near impossible for you to plow through the mud and filth to find the clean spots of truth hidden therein. That is why your heart must be guarded carefully.

The heart is a precious thing: it is the most priceless part of you because through it, I work with you and I speak to you. All I have ever said to you is written in your heart. Search it to find the truths written there even before you were born. If you are in touch with your heart and its deep yearnings, then you will truly find me and understand what I am saying to you. You will know the things I have placed there for you to fathom and unravel as you travel on your life's journey. They will guide you and lead you along the road that you should take.

You cannot depend on anyone else to do that for you. You alone are responsible. In your heart alone, have they been placed. The secrets hidden within you are yours to find out and no one else. That is why at times you need to take yourself away from the crowd and the distractions, and search deep within. That is why the depths of the ocean and greatness of the mountains beckons you quietly to come away to yourself and find me, the me hidden within you through my Holy Spirit.

I want you: I desire you: I want you to find me that you might manifest my glory to the world ... my glory that I have placed within you. It is within you, but not of you. That is why it is difficult to find or to contend with. That is why you have to search for it, and that is why there is conflict and struggle within and without. I have written it and placed it within you, separate and apart from the flesh you are made of. But the world system only teaches you to develop the 'you' that pertains to the mind and the flesh, so your spirit lies dead within you and the things that pertain to it lie dormant and undeveloped.

I have placed a spirit life within each of you, and although it lies dormant and lifeless, once you find me and begin to listen to me, it will come to life, and will guide you throughout your years … only if your spirit connects with mine.

The sea is your tutor; it is for your inspiration. Its depth beckons you and speaks to you of the indefinable and unsearchable depths of my Spirit. Know that if I created the depths of the ocean and the expanse of the heavens, know that my own wisdom and greatness surpasses it by as many tines as you can imagine the vastness and unending stretch of the deeps. I am wider and broader and deeper and higher than anything you can conceive of.

I Am Always There

The days will come when you forget me, when you become busy or sick, and other things seem to take priority above me. But I am still there waiting for you – waiting for a re-connection with you. For truly my Spirit, within you, is restless, and stands waiting for me too. So there is longing on both sides for the reunion and for the restoration of the intimacy we lost. So you become restless and miserable and don't know why. But it is because you miss me as much as I miss you.

You must get your mind adjusted to the thought that you will never be yourself – be totally comfortable with who you are or where you are – until you become intimately connected with me. Once you have tasted the joy of the union that comes when you share intimacy with me, you will know what you desired and missed.

I recognize your distractions sometimes, and the occasional fears and doubts you have, and often I do not judge you because I understand the dichotomy you experience … you are made in my image, but you are human. I understand the polarization. I understand more than you ever dream or imagine. I understand fully well all that you go through – all the decisions you have to make, all the corners you have to turn, and all the diversions you have to contend with. I understand fully.

And so I want you to turn back to me and seek me with all your heart, so that I can help you. Seek me as of vital necessity for your life. I am always waiting for you to come back and will embrace you with my warmth, and fulfill your deepest desires. But if you don't turn back to me, then I cannot help you – at all – no matter how much I want to.

So come into my arms now, and enjoy my fullness. Come running wholeheartedly into my arms and I will embrace you with my love. But *you* must come; you have to come.

You think I don't understand, or that I get easily impatient with you as man does, but I don't. My patience, my mercy or my loving-kindness never ends. It never ends for you because I love you dearly and sincerely with all my heart. Yes, my love is universal, but I want you to know that I delight in you, my child. I delight in your presence. I delight when you turn to me and come running back to me. I take pleasure in you my beloved.

My Kingdom is Infinite

My kingdom is infinite. It knows no beginning or ending. It is forever, lasting throughout eternity. So whatever relates to my kingdom is of eternal value. That is why it is so important to find your place in its establishment. And that is my purpose for you here and now … to secure for you, a place in my everlasting kingdom.

Your desires, your thoughts, your actions and your beliefs determine if you have a place in my kingdom, or not. And I tell you plainly there is a place for all who will turn to me … those who will step away from the things of this world that consume them and their time and energy, and turn towards my kingdom.

Remember, I say, you must enter my kingdom as a little child. You should seek to learn of me and my ways like how a child – a baby learns of the ways of its mother. So you must turn to me when you enter my kingdom. See it … consider it as the beginning of a new life for you. You must learn like a child how to walk and talk and think. Like a child, you must seek earnestly to learn what life in the Kingdom of God is all about. Seek to understand its culture and how you are expected to live and walk each day in your life.

Like a child imitates his parents, so you must imitate me – even when sometimes you don't quite understand what you are doing, or why you are required to do some things. Like a child, you must just do it, just because you trust me, and I say it is so, or I say you must do it.

At times, you may fall, and fail and even judge me because you do not fully understand the way I think and perceive things, or because you don't have a grasp of the inexhaustibleness of my wisdom and knowledge. So, sometimes my actions might seem harsh and cruel to you, and you want to rebel. Sometimes you might even hate me and curse me in your heart like your children do to you.

But know that that is how it must be because you will never fully understand my ways until the end. You will never be able to fully grasp everything until then, so just trust me.

Yes, you will mature in me and begin to understand some of the deep things of the Spirit, some of the deep things hidden from the foundation of the world. I will share them with you and reveal my heart to you so that you will begin to know me more. And as you begin to know me more and love me with greater passion, your faith will grow and you will begin to experience me in a new and deeper way. I look forward to an increasingly deep and intimate relationship with you. Then I will reveal myself to you as you become more and more unhindered by the things of the flesh, and you press in unencumbered to see my face and to know me.

Above all, I look forward to that day when eternity will be clear to you who are born of my own spirit and blood. I look forward to intimacy with you as you take up your position as kings and priests in my kingdom.

Then, there will be no line of demarcation separating us, then, you will come directly into my presence and see me face to face, as I see you today. Then you will know me as I know you.

Disappointments

When disappointments come your way, turn to me and trust in me. I am still there, standing right behind you, beside you, waiting and looking and hoping for your attention and your focus. I am there willing you to understand that I am with you in it all, in everything, good and bad.

You have to see me there with you, sharing all that you are going through, knowing that you do feel hurt, pain and loss. I am there even when you don't seem to see me.

If you would just trust me, you would be able to see me, and as you look into my eyes and catch a glimpse of my heart you would begin to understand what I am doing. I want you to understand. I want you to know my heart and my way so that we can laugh and smile together as we grow to understand each other… even in the pains and hurts of your life.

I have chosen you that you might know me intimately, that you might know my heart and my ways, and even my thoughts. I want to make them known to you that you might have good success in me. If you try, you will. You will know me if you persevere, if you see me in all that happens to you, even all your cross and pain. If you would know me, you would.

In your heart there are doubts and fears about me. But it is because you don't know me, why you fear me. If you knew me, you would sense the love I have in my heart for you and the pain I feel for you. You would know my desire for you, to heal you and fill you, and fulfill you. You would know my love and compassion for you.

If you would trust me, your pain would go, all the agony and the pain and grief. I would fill you … fill that gap. If you would know me, I would fill you full with my love and my knowledge. If you desire me with all your heart, you would know me and love me more. You would trust me and believe in me, in all that I say and all that I am.

I would love you and draw you close to me in my arms and fill you – cover you with my love so that you would not be afraid.

I Never Sleep

I never sleep or grow weary: I always see: my eyes and my ears are always open to the cry of my own. I listen and I hear, but I have a time – a time for everything under heaven.

I know what is right and wrong; I know when you are ready to hear and to do too. I am God. I am today what I was yesterday; I am forever. So listen to me. Trust in me always.

In your eyes, it seems like at times, I rouse myself as out of a stupor. But that is not so because I AM. I always hear and I always see. I care, really care and understand, but I have a time and season for all things. I cannot act before the fullness of time: I cannot act before you are ready.

I know all things, I understand all things, and I do all things well, so when I act it is good and right. Only then is it right: when I do it. I cannot be wrong, I cannot be out of tune or out of time. The right time is when I say it and do it. That is what makes it right – not the seeming concurrences of events and situations. I am the one who initiates those seeming twists of fate … those coincidences. I cause them and that's what gives them validity. The coincidences of themselves don't make things right. It is because I coordinate and orchestrate them that make them right.

I am the author of all things, and I am a good God. When you pray to me you do not change my mind. My mind cannot change since I see it all before it is conceived in the natural. That is why you should seek to pray according to my will. My will always prevails.

Don't try to change my mind, unless you know my heart and will and desire. If you walk in my will then you will know the things I want and desire for you, and you will get them then because when you pray you will pray according to my will.

Yes, I am in charge. I own all things and can do all things. But for me to work on your behalf, you have to yield your will to mine.

The truth is that when you are mine, your very desires emanate from me. The dreams and aspirations in your heart come from me and so do the fulfillment of them … all of them. I am the author of your thoughts; I created your mind, your heart, your intellect. I have designed them specifically to suit you – so you can become the person I meant you to be. So, all the glory belongs to me. Any glory you get reflects back on me, and belongs to me because you cannot contain it in yourself. It is mine. Give it back to me, and then you will prosper and succeed.

I have given you the tools needed to bring to fruition that dream and desire in you. But you have to take up the tools and begin the work of fulfilling that which you have in your heart. You work and I fashion the design from the blueprint that I alone possess. It is my responsibility to accomplish it. You plant the physical seed through your work, and I make it grow. Your seed is to go and do.

Waiting

There is really no such thing as waiting in my kingdom. There is just the element of timing. So when I say you are to wait on me, I mean you are to live according to what my word teaches and how your heart guides you until your change comes. There are times and periods to do different things and to be different things. The thing for you is to make sure that you are doing what you should be doing at the right time. Trust me and do what is at hand for you to do, and let go.

Do not fret or worry over the things I tell you will come to pass. Just prepare yourself and live your life to the fullest. Live as if it is your last day, each day and so you won't have the feeling – the sense of waiting.

Just do what I tell you to do, listen as I speak, and I will guide you. That is all you need to do. Live to the fullest each day. Do not grow weary with your time or with what you are doing. If you are alert, if you live in my presence you will know when your change comes. It will just overtake you unexpectedly. But you must be doing at all times – doing the thing for the moment, in the moment, at the moment, and I will fulfill your call.

I will do the fulfilling, if you are ready and in the right place and doing the right thing. You wouldn't have been waiting; you would have been living.

You are your greatest enemy when you watch the time and the clock, thinking about all the things that could be done and should be done. That takes away time from your work. Just do the little you are called to do and it will fit into the whole mosaic of life and time.

Trust me. I have made the pattern: I have designed the patchwork. I know when and where each piece fits in, I alone. So don't judge yourself by what other people are doing with and in their lives at a particular time. They cannot really accomplish anything of value outside of their time. Anything done outside of my design does not count. It is of no real value. So be careful that you do not end up wasting your time by being busy and doing the wrong thing at the wrong time or the right thing at the wrong time just to please others or receive praise from man.

Trust me; trust in me. Remain steadfast in me and all things will work out for your good. That is of paramount importance: trust in me. I will work it out even when it seems impossible and improbable.

I, for my part, have trusted you with my word, the word that I placed within you. I expect you to keep it within you and store it in your heart, knowing that I am faithful to what I say. Everything will happen in its season … everything … if you trust me. That is the covenant I make with you: trust in me and I will bring it to pass always, always. Just trust in me.

If you think I am slack in bringing to pass the things I say, then you don't know me or truly trust me, and this should be the essence of our relationship. That is the reason I have called you to be my torchbearers. It is based on your acknowledgement of who I am … that I am God who cannot fail or grow weary or faint.

You are my light here in this world and it is I who keep your light burning to carry the news and do the work I have placed within you. Trust in me is all you need.

Waiting is like the time it takes a plant to grow from a seed to the fruit-bearing tree it becomes at maturity. Different trees take different times, and need different types of soil to thrive. Generally, trees are not good or bad in themselves: there are only trees that fulfill their purpose and trees that don't. No tree can carry a fruit that it was not designed to carry, or bear fruit out of its season, unless I do it for a special end … to tell a story.

So even though, with the natural eye a tree doesn't seem to be bearing fruit, as long as it is still grounded in the soil, the source from which it receives its sustenance, it is still alive and well. It is still fruitful in my sight.

Fruitful, to me, is doing what you should be doing and being where you should be at the right time. You don't cut down a tree when its period of fruitfulness is past for a season. You tend it and prune it, if needs be, until its time of year returns. So, although it is not fruitful to you when you can't see the fruits on its branches, to me it is productive because it is at the point where it should be at the appropriate time.

The reason why my Son cursed the fig tree was that it wasn't bearing fruit during its seasonal period of fruitfulness – when the master needed return it was not able to fulfill its sole purpose for existence.

God of the Marketplace

I am the God of the quiet Sunday morning, but I am also the God of the marketplace.

You have caused the church experience to give others a false impression of who I really am. You give the impression that I am not a God of the marketplace or of the workaday world. You convey the sense that I am not able to handle the grit and the grime, or the dust and dirt of the routine activities of your daily life.

You make me come across as a puny God, who is found only in places of soft music and dim lights, a God whom you have to dress up daintily in your finery to come to. You treat me like I am a delicate God who can't handle your everyday attire. You make it seem I am only available to meet with you when you are all dressed up in your finery, and all the other times you are on your own.

You close your eyes when you worship and when you pray making it seem that I am not really here in the midst of your activities and deliberations, in your courts, shops, businesses or the construction undertaken daily in life. It's okay to close your eyes, but don't forget that while your spirit might easier connect to me when you close your eyes to blot out the distractions of the world, I am also right in the midst of you in every situation.

So I require that you present me in a different configuration today. I want you to make me seem as I really am: a hardworking and powerful God with muscles, a God who is able to tackle the stresses, fights and struggles of everyday life. I am the God who rolls up his sleeves and enters into the brawls and confrontations of your daily life.

Even the very music you use to worship me sometimes seems so dull and tuneless. It seems to say that I am a God who belongs to a different age: I am a God for whom you have to bend over backwards in order to identify with. You deal with me with me like how you deal with your aged and obsolete grandparents, who are unfamiliar with the things and ways of modern life. You seek to please and entertain them in your off moments just because you are caring and considerate of the weak and aging. So in moments of kindness and reminiscence you will play their music and do their dance to make them happy. And when you are ready to live a normal life again – to return to your daily routine, and do what modern people do, you have to sideline them out of necessity – not that you really want to but life simply demands that you leave them behind. It's not their fault, but the fact is that they are ancient, and they no longer fit in or understand contemporary life and the changes that occur daily. They are not able to grasp the ideas and customs of the modern world, so now the parent-child roles are reversed and you are in charge. You are now in control of circumstances so you watch over them, and out of kindness and compassion, you seek to defend them in their old-fashioned ways. You lovingly protect them because they are yours, but kind of archaic.

That is the way many of you now deal with me. Deep down, you think you are in charge and it's your responsibility to shield this defunct and old-fashioned God. But I require that you change that image of me today.

I will be represented in a new way. There is a changing of the guard. I must be shown to be the Lord of the age, the initiator of ideas – the one who determines the outcome of the path that society takes. I am the defender and the originator – not the one to be defended.

Some of the things, the forms and structures, you are holding on to must go to suit the present life. They must not change to amuse or please, but to rightly represent the God of the marketplace and the God of the struggles and stresses you face in everyday life.

I am God, the contender, who fights battles and will not relent or give in to man's arrogance and humanistic ways, or to man's rebellion and disregard for my laws and precepts. I must be seen and known as the God who will not bend back or bow to the vicissitudes of this life.

I am God and will be seen as the one in charge, a God in full control. I am the God who determines the paths and the ways that man must take. You must change the way you present me so that others might see me for who I am, and be drawn to me and come to know me, the only true God.

That means you have to set aside the conventions and teachings of man and his traditions, and go back to my word with a fresh ear to hear what I am now saying. It's like the time of Christ when the religious leaders of the day lauded and honored the traditions of their elders, and condemned the teaching and practices of Jesus and his disciples because they did not fast – fasting was the good and right thing to do. Jesus responded with a very short parable. You cannot put new wine in old wineskins, or the old wineskins will burst. New wine needs new bottles.

Perseverance

Diligence, excellence, perfection! Go after those things, pursue them. Go after the things you want but don't lose hope when they seem to elude you. Have regard for perseverance.

The things you desire will not come together all at once. Every great pursuit demands time and patience. Perseverance is one of my own attributes, and I have bequeathed that to you, personally. Perseverance is how you will testify of me – that you didn't give up when faced with obstacles … when impossibilities seemed to abound.

I want you to talk about the times when the stars seemed unreachable – even the top of the trees seemed beyond your grasp. Talk about how you persisted, how you persevered, how you kept on. That will bear testimony to my own perseverance. Do not shun tests and trials; do not be afraid of them or of telling about the times when you were pressed to the limit. Do not deny them. Perseverance is of me, and it becomes you. It is a measure of how much you are being transformed into my image, the image of Christ on earth. It is an attribute to you and it is beautiful in my sight.

And that is why you will be tested and tried until the knowledge you have of me in your head becomes knowledge of the heart, and you become more like my Son.

New Beginnings

I still need those who will be my mouthpiece and speak on my behalf. I still need those with a heart after my own heart, who will seek truth and an understanding of the purity of my word. I need those who will seek me to know my inclinations and my desire and to discern the things I want to accomplish in such a time as this.

This is a new age, a new era, a new season. The things that were valued and esteemed in times just past, will no longer be considered so significant. The things that men pursued, looked up to and looked forward to, will no longer delude or entice them. They will begin to seek something new that is not of this world ... my kingdom. They will want to know my heart and what I think, and how to know me. They will want to know me and see my face.

This is a time of new beginnings all around. New beginnings in the system, new beginnings in the arena, new beginnings in your personal life. I am doing something new: new to you. I will be calling you to work with me in accomplishing the things I want to be done. You will hear my voice distinctly and understand clearly what I speak. You will know my meaning and my heart when I reveal to you truths about establishing my kingdom here on earth.

My kingdom will be known by all. They will see my power, my might and my strength. Many will know me and bow down to worship me. They will see my face and honor me because I am their God. They will know me … really know me.

Time for Me

At long last you have found time for me again … time to sit with me and talk with me and enjoy my presence without interference. I long for those moments with you when we sit alone together and converse with each other from one heart to another.

I love your heart and when you seek after me. It is my delight to spend time with you and get to know you more as you open yourself to me. It is my delight and my joy when you put everything aside and seek my presence. I love you dearly for these few moments together.

You are precious to me in every way – ways that you don't even dream of, ways that seem simple and unimportant. But they matter to me and to us – our relationship. You are precious in my sight more than you imagine. I like when your heart is after me, and when you delight in me and seek to know my word and to do it.

I like your desire to please me intensely: your passion and your fervor for me. They mean much to me and they make you dear to me.

Come sit with me and I will tell you what things must be … how you will conquer the foe and succeed. You will make it… you will make it in the path I have set out for you. You will accomplish it without fail, if you seek after me, and I will be faithful to my word … faithful to all I say will come to pass.

You are more than dear to me when you are diligent in seeking my ways. You will hear my heart and know me because you pursue me and you love the things I admire.

Know this, I see you amid the crowd and laughter. I take note of you in the midst of the business and all the activities. I watch over you and keep my eye on you because you are my own.

I want to be with you as much as you want to be with me. I want your close attention and your focus on what I am doing and saying. Your vital attention is necessary, is very important at this time for I am speaking … speaking volumes about what is, and what is to be.

You are to listen and take seriously, not just gloss over what I am saying or take it lightly. It is of eternal value. I will work in you to bring out the things I have placed in you. I will bring them into being – everything. Take me seriously and move. Do it. Do what comes to you. Do it willingly and gladly. It will bear fruit in you and through you.

You are to observe what and where I send you. You are to notice what I do and what is happening around you. Take it seriously. Take yourself seriously.

The thing you desire and the dreams you have are real. I placed them inside of you; I am the one in charge of your life and I do not waver or change. I am not double-minded and neither should you. I am consistent and deliberate; I act with purpose and deliberateness. I am not a slight God – I don't do things lightly, but with passion and purpose.

Follow my example, take yourself seriously and act with confidence and authority. You have me behind you and with you, even in front of you. I am your example, your kinsman. I want you to follow me and imitate me with all fervor and passion so you will excel.

You have the passion and the drive to succeed. You have my drive and passion within you. Get up and walk with purpose and deliberation. Show yourself for what you are in me.

Eternal Laws

I decided even before you sinned, that I would die for you. That I would come down to earth myself and take the punishment that was inevitable for the crime done.

I know it is hard for you to understand what I am saying, especially when you look at what is happening around you and see even the small or sometimes great tragedies in your own life your family, friends, and the world at large.

But what you have to understand is that when I created the universe, I put natural laws in place and they are untenable. You cannot wish them away, you simple cannot change them. If you think about it yourself, you will realize that if the natural laws changed willy-nilly, then there would be no science, and life would be total confusion. You simply could not plan from one day to the next.

For instance, just as you cannot change the law of gravity, so you cannot change other laws I have put in place. If you jump from a thirty storey floor, you will crash to the ground and die, whether you intended to kill yourself or not. So it is when the first man disobeyed my law, there were consequences, which I told him about. It was a law. So instantly he died spiritually and the process of natural death, which I warned him about, was activated.

You have to understand that my word is law. Whatever I speak comes to pass. Even now, you exist on this earth which spins on its own axis by the power of my spoken word. My word can never die or lose its power. So that is why I have given you the Holy Bible to live by, my word and my laws, which man has written through the inspiration of my Holy Spirit.

My word is truth and cannot change, whether you believe it or not, or whether you accept it or not. It is just a fact of life that you have to live with. That is why I appeal to you to come to me, follow my word – get to know me, know my heart that you might have understanding and good success.

Beware of Deception

How long have you heard of me and the things I have done for others? Or how long have you wanted to know me but have never called out to me? And others of you, how long have you known me but for some unexplained reason you have broken your trust with me? I testify before you that I have not broken trust with you. It was you who lost your way; you took a wrong turn and abandoned me.

But I understand your struggle and your propensity to wander, so I stand right beside you waiting for you call out to me and turn back to me.

You wonder why King Asa of Israel turned to man for help and counsel after knowing me and trusting me for 36 years. The answer is that he had gown complacent during 25 years of uninterrupted peace; he had forgotten to call upon me, and when the time of need came he became weary and took what he thought was the easy way out; he chose to act on natural instinct. He remembered what his father had done, and followed him. It was because during that time of peace and ease, the enemy came in and deceived the king.

King Asa by then had won many battles with my help, and I had given him peace from his enemies for 25 years. At that time, he had sought me wholehearted and even deposed his own mother-in-law, who had turned her back on me. But after 25 years, when war started again, Asa felt disinclined to fight. He might have felt that by then, he understood kingship, or he might have simply felt too old or too weak to fight and decided there was an easier way than combat. But he did not turn to me for help or counsel. Instead, he did what his sinful father had done, and turned to man in his time of trouble.

But you take care. At times when your flesh feels tired and weary, you might become confused and allow the enemy to come in and take advantage of you. The enemy makes it seem easier to trust in man who you can see with the natural eye, than to exercise faith and maintain your trust in me. But it is only a deception of the enemy to make the solution to your problem seem surer and more secure when you give in to the persuasion of the flesh.

In truth, what you don't realize is that in those times when you feel weak and flustered, or when you feel you are at the end and can't go any further, it is much easier for you to tap into my resources than when you feel strong and secure. My hands always remain outstretched and waiting for you to reach out to me: like when Peter began to sink after walking on the water.

Imagine that your own son or daughter is sinking in quicksand or hanging from a half-broken limb, and you tell your falling child to stretch his hand to reach you. If the child stretches his hand, you instantly grab on to it with all your strength because your arm is already outstretched waiting anxiously and nervously for that hand. And with joy and relief, you hold on with all your strength to that son or daughter until you have pulled him to safety. But, if that son or daughter does not stretch out his hand to you as you instruct him, he will sink; he will fall or go under that quicksand even though you are right there in his presence waiting to save him.

So it is with me. So I pray of you, learn to call out to me as your first response to every situation. Practice doing it daily, in every circumstance, in every situation so when the temptations come, reaching out to me is the most natural response in the world.

And even if you miss it once, don't let the enemy bash you on the head and keep you down. Repent and turn back. Don't let pride draw you further away, like Asa who became angry with the prophet who chastised him. His heart became so hardened after a time that he even refused to think of turning to me for healing when he became sick in the foot and no one else could help. He was so deceived by the enemy that he would rather die than turn to me for healing.

I beg of you do not be deceived: know that we have a common enemy whose sole desire is to destroy you because you are the apple of my eye. He is jealous of you. I am your friend.

Nirvana

Outside of me, your creator, your life has no real meaning. It is just a chasing after the wind.

You were created for one ultimate purpose, and that is to serve your creator: to pursue him and do what he says in order to fulfill the design and plan he has for your individual life. Aside from that, any happiness you experience is not real joy or happiness. It is simply a man-created state of Nirvana to numb the senses that you are living a completely meaningless life.

If your creator discounts what you are doing, then it is of absolutely no real value; your work is going to be destroyed and burnt up at the end of time. It simply means that you are living in a state of self-delusion.

I know your reasoning: you say after you die nothing matters; therefore all is well as long as you are honoured for your work and your gifts now, when you are alive. But I say to you, you will stand before me in judgement, every one of you. Every man woman and child was born with an eternal spirit inside of the shell of your body. It is not your body that makes you human; it is that spirit, my spirit which I breathed into before your creation. That is why whether you are born blind, or deaf, or mute, or with a malformed shape or a disease, you are still mankind because you have my breath within you. And that spirit within you can never die. That spirit within you lives forever.

So at the end of your life, even though your flesh will perish and go back to the earth from which I made it, your spirit does not remain with the decaying flesh. Your spirit returns to me from whence it came, and spirits don't die. So you are destined to live with me eternally, or to live in torment, apart from me forever.

I know your thinking and my heart grieves for you; I know some of you have chosen in your heart to believe a lie, and others of you are battling it out in your heart what to believe. You want to believe in me your creator, but the learned of the world tell you, you are simple-minded and foolish, if you do. They tell you I do not exist: they tell you, you happened by chance, by a process of evolution; they tell you are flesh and no spirit, and when you die there is no further life for you.

But I challenge you today, what will you believe? Who will you believe? I am the eternal God. I was from the beginning. I AM the beginning: there is no beginning outside of me, and I have no ending. I have seen all the ages past before your time: I see all things and I know all things. I possess all wisdom and knowledge. Your scientists, and thinkers and all your great men have come and gone. They have spent their years studying the universe and the order I have put in place. They can't create air or atoms or rocks or sea or mountains or sky, or any life form. They merely observe what I have created and present their observations to you from their limited perspective of the time and period in which they live. But I was before all, and I will outlast all.

So whom will you believe – a created man with the same brain and intellect and feelings as your own – a man who will pass away in the same way that you will – or will you believe me? I know the measure of the seas, I know the depths of the oceans and the expanse of the skies. I know who will live and who will die, and when you will die.

I want you to believe me because I love you, and I have eternal life for you. I promise you the life that you desire way deep down inside of you, but which you cannot experience on this present earth because of sin. I promise you the life that you dream of, with love and peace and harmony and beauty. I promise you heaven, but I also promise you a new earth which will never pass away. It will be an earth with cities and life, real life, except without the evil.

No, you will not be only drinking milk and honey, but you will be able to feast at my table; you will have abundant life. I will not take away the gifts and talents I have given to you. You will have all the opportunity to use them and to work in my kingdom.

Test Administrator

Even though I don't initiate all your tests, I administer them, and that is why I tell you, you will never be tested more than you can bear. I allow your tests that you can be changed. I know exactly what problems you will face, and I also know the solution to each problem.

When my chosen people were going through the wilderness I led them with a cloud by day and a pillar of fire by night. I knew all their needs including their need for food and water. And I allowed them to go for three days without water, but not one of them died from dehydration. I know the make-up of your body, and that in the natural, from your estimation, three days is as long as you can go without water. But I was determined to test them, to make them know what was in their own heart.

Whenever I test, it is always that you can learn. I already know all the answers. I already know your heart and what you really are, but I want you to know that you have the opportunity to confess and repent so that you might become who you were designed to be.

I allowed them to go for three days without water, and when they did find water it was bitter. I know that in the natural it seems extreme to you, and perhaps heartless. It appears as if I was not with them, or I had forgotten them. I know form a human perspective that test might seem too great to bear. Surely, you think they would be at the point of collapse. But I want you to know that desperate situations like these bring out the thoughts that are deep in the heart as you begin to speak in anger and frustration. And in your heart you often blame me, even though like the children of Israel who blamed Moses, you might outwardly blame man.

And I know that in your eyes, their anger is justified since they were led in a situation which they did not create, and which they were unable to change: they were helpless as far as finding water was concerned. And that is the time that anger rages inside of you, when you feel trapped and imprisoned in circumstances you did not choose, and you can't do anything in the natural to change.

Then Moses cries out to me in desperation, and all he has to do is throw a piece of stick in the water, and bitter water becomes sweet.

Why did I allow them to get to such a desperate point as a nation of people ... to get to the point of almost death? It is because I wanted them, like I want you, to get to the end of themselves ... the end of relying on the mind and on the flesh. You have to get to the end of yourself, open your eyes and turn to me, and I will show you the way. And how do you know when you are at the end of yourself? When you cannot go on any further without me ... when the test affects your life itself. Then you must turn to me because you cannot help yourself. It is that test that I use to change you that you might become what you were intended to be ... priests and kings in my kingdom.

Parables

Why do I speak in parables? Why do I explain my Kingdom in metaphors? Because the secrets of my kingdom are reserved for those who diligently search for it. I choose to reveal myself to those who take time out to seek me and to know my heart ... to those who seek to dwell in my secret place.

I have counseled you: do not throw pearls before swine or they will trample the pearls and turn around and come after you. By that I mean you are to give what is precious only to those who are ready to receive it. If you have my discernment, you will know when to share your pearls with those who are hungry for something more. And so I practice this counsel I give to you.

My kingdom is the mother of all pearls. It is that supreme pearl for which the seeker of pearls will sell all the others he has found to acquire that one superior pearl, which he will treasure and hold dear to his heart for the rest of his life. My kingdom is the treasure hidden in a field for which the one who seeks after treasures will sell all the other treasures he has amassed to secure that greatest of all treasures. Knowledge of my kingdom is precious; it is reserved for those who are truly and sincerely in search of the King.

I know how your heart works; I know how lightly and carelessly you regard those things that come easily to you. I understand the spirit of inquiry which I have placed within you. I understand your desire to be challenged and to pursue that which seems out of your grasp – that which stretches you to your very limit.

Such is the pursuit of my kingdom. It will take you all of your whole lifetime and more because my kingdom is unfathomable and inexhaustible. It is eternal and infinite while your mind is finite. That is why in order to begin to understand my kingdom you have to devote your entire being…your body, mind and spirit to its pursuit.

I tell you that that anyone who enters my kingdom and turns back is not worthy of it: the pursuit of me and my kingdom must come before husband, wife, mother, father, children and all those who are dear and precious to you. Only in such determined pursuit of me and my kingdom and its secrets, will any man or woman ever begin to have any kind of true intimacy with me, or begin to understand my heart and my ways. And in your sincere pursuit of me, I will in turn look after you and your own, and give back to you, those things that will fulfill you, so you will experience my goodness.